Gendered Marketing

T0327393

GENDERED MANAGEMENT

Gendered Management is a curated series of authored books which take key management concepts and explore them explicitly from a feminist perspective. Grounded in research, but accessible for students, these books will challenge conventional thinking across all areas of management. Written by authors with a strong publications record, these books aim to reframe debates across business and management theory, teaching and practice.

Gendered Marketing

Pauline Maclaran

Professor of Marketing and Consumer Research, Department of Marketing, Royal Holloway, University of London, UK

Andreas Chatzidakis

Professor in Marketing, Department of Marketing, Royal Holloway, University of London, UK

GENDERED MANAGEMENT

Edward Elgar
PUBLISHING

Cheltenham, UK • Northampton, MA, USA

Published by
Edward Elgar Publishing Limited
The Lypiatts
15 Lansdown Road
Cheltenham
Glos GL50 2JA
UK

Edward Elgar Publishing, Inc.
William Pratt House
9 Dewey Court
Northampton
Massachusetts 01060
USA

Paperback edition 2023

A catalogue record for this book
is available from the British Library

Library of Congress Control Number: 2022938785

This book is available electronically in the **Elgar**online
Business subject collection
http://dx.doi.org/10.4337/9781839108822

ISBN 978 1 83910 881 5 (cased)
ISBN 978 1 83910 882 2 (eBook)
ISBN 978 1 0353 1692 2 (paperback)

Printed and bound by CPI Group (UK) Ltd, Croydon, CR0 4YY

Contents

Figures

1. Introduction: an overview of gendered marketing

Contemporary consumer culture is overflowing with pointlessly gendered products: pink and purple BIC pens for women, Kleenex 'mansize' tissues, Gillette's men's and women's razors are but a few. And Chick Beer, with its promise of less bloating, is possibly the strongest contender for the silly prize. Products like these – so obviously gendered for little reason – feed a never-ending stream of mocking memes on social media, but they only represent the tip of the gendered marketing iceberg. Markets and the marketing activities that sustain them are frequently riddled with ideological biases reinforcing inequality across public and private domains, biases that affect our cultural perceptions of what it means to be male, female or non-binary. Of course, marketing activities can also challenge gender prejudices or misconceptions about particular groups if used creatively and in transformative ways. Yet, the countering of gender biases remains limited, tending to arise only when a group has economic power such as the so-called 'pink pound', a phrase used since the 1980s to describe the purchasing power of the LGBTQI+ community. Markets and money talk! Too often equality depends on access to economic resources.

Our intention with this book is to make an in-depth exploration of the gendered nature of marketing theory and practice, to unpack the many ideological assumptions embedded in marketing thought and action. We do this from the position of marketing scholars who also hold feminist views, a position we believe enables us to better understand some of subtleties at work in the gendering of marketing (and the marketing of gender). Our exploration draws on current and past scholarship at the intersection of marketing and feminism, as well as featuring core bodies of feminist theorising with relevance for the questioning of marketing knowledge. Before undertaking a more detailed analysis of the specific areas around which the book is structured – the history of marketing thought, communications, product design and branding, marketing's free externalities and the marketing organisation – this introductory chapter gives a brief summary of the field to date and outlines key feminist theories used in the chapters that follow.

WHY FEMINISM?

Often referred to colloquially as the 'F' word, feminism stirs many emotions in both its supporters and detractors. In fact, as Sarah Banet-Weiser (2018) insightfully highlights in her recent book on current gender politics, the rise of popular feminism has been paralleled by a rise in popular misogyny with, for example, websites such as *The Red Pill*,[1] an online community hosted by Reddit where men voice their toxic views on women's empowerment and much more. However, feminism is not about women hating men (misandry) or wanting to oppress men. At its core, feminism seeks social, political and economic equality for women as well as men, aims that are perfectly reasonable and legitimate in order to have a satisfactory human existence for all. In order to achieve these aims feminists strive to expose the barriers to women's advancement, raise awareness of inequalities and campaign for measures to right the imbalances. Feminism therefore has two main strands that interweave and inform one another: feminist scholarship and feminist social movements. Together they cover not only theories, but also practices and politics to achieve equality for women (Hearn and Hein, 2015).

So where does marketing come into this? The answer is complex and not just the obvious empowerment messages that pervade marketing communications targeted at female segments. Certainly marketing's empowering slogans have done much to raise the profile of feminism and, indeed, to make it highly visible. But the chief message – that you can buy your way to independence – is often voiced at the expense of any wider structural critique that questions patriarchal values embedded in all major social institutions, namely family, government, the economy, religion and education. Marketing activities and systems reflect these social institutions and are often unknowingly gendered in a myriad of ways that this book will endeavour to reveal. The next section looks at where we've come from in this respect, tracking the evolution of feminist thought and its critique of market-related structures and activities.

EARLY FEMINIST SCHOLARSHIP IN MARKETING

Although marketing scholars acknowledged feminism as early as 1972 when Alice Beery undertook a survey to explore women's views of feminist movements with a view to better promote their cause, it would take nearly another 20 years before feminist critique entered marketing and consumer research scholarship. Prior to this there had been many feminist voices criticising marketing from outside the discipline. Betty Friedan's (1963) polemic, *The Feminine Mystique*, railed against the patriarchal forces controlling women through domesticity, and implicated marketing and advertising as key forces in this respect. Jean Kilbourne's pioneering film, *Killing Us Softly* (1979), castigated advertisers for their demeaning and dehumanising portrayals of women. And more widely, during the 1970s and 1980s, feminism took a strong anti-market stance, even while many such as Kilbourne used its methods to publicise and brand their messages and ideas.

Significant feminist critiques within marketing appeared from the 1990s onwards. On account of the emphasis that feminist principles place on the interconnectedness of knowledge together with interdisciplinary approaches, feminism sat well with the emerging interpretivist research paradigm of the time. Initially feminist marketing scholars exposed how marketing discourse itself was gendered, often privileging masculine rather than feminine characteristics and values (Costa, 1991; Bristor and Fischer, 1993; Hirschman, 1993). Subsequently, various studies revealed the gendered nature of the consumer subject position (Fischer and Bristor, 1994) as well as the many ways advertising contributed to gender stereotypes (Stern, 1993). By 2000 there was sufficient work for an edited collection, *Marketing and Feminism* by Catterall, Maclaran and Stevens. In contrast to feminists from other disciplines, what feminist scholars from within marketing were able to unpack was the intricate entanglements of markets in women's everyday lives, whether these exacerbated ideologies of intensive mothering or encouraged women to find their own unique self-expression. Linda Scott, in her ground-breaking book, *Fresh Lipstick*, critiqued the conventional feminist reduction of fashion to sexual objectification, a stance, she argued, that was about control and exclusion of other women. This focus on appearance impeded the movement's progress to achieve its true aims of equality for all women around the globe (Scott, 2005). To this end, Linda herself has worked tirelessly with women in developing economies to close the gender gap through female entrepreneurship, work culminating in her most recent text, *The Double X Economy* (Scott, 2020) and to which we will return later.

Nevertheless, despite all of this initial feminist momentum in marketing and consumer research, there was something of a hiatus in feminist perspectives as broader identity politics came to the fore. Looking back, it seems that critique became muted by the celebration of difference that grew in tandem with a pervasive neoliberal ideology and the 'new spirit of capitalism' (Boltanski and Chiapello, 2007).

THE CURRENT STATE OF PLAY

Now, over the last decade, we see a steady resurrection of feminist voices in marketing and consumer research, particularly among younger scholars, an interest sparked by the realisation that not much has changed from a wider, structural perspective. Women continue to receive less pay for the same work as their male colleagues and are still largely absent from boardrooms and top positions. High-profile movements like #metoo and #timesup have also fuelled interest, alongside recent feminist scholarship that heavily critiques the role of the market in appropriating feminist messages of empowerment, leading to a type of neoliberal feminism that mutes feminism's collective force in favour of white, middle-class, professional women (Banet-Weiser, 2018; Rottenberg, 2018).

Within marketing, the focus on the role of the market in gender (in) justice has intensified with studies revealing insights about the marketisation of women's empowerment and the global gender asymmetries in marketing and consumer behaviour (Hein et al., 2016). Even marketing initiatives designed to do good – i.e. social marketing campaigns or fairtrade schemes – may be misaligned with the embodied realities of producers and consumers in emerging economies. Such studies have prompted renewed calls to make gender visible and to identify gender power within heteronormativity, racialisation, embodiments, spatialisations, virtualisation and transnationalisations; all fields of increasing relevance to markets (Hearn and Hein, 2015).

INFLUENTIAL FEMINIST PERSPECTIVES IN MARKETING

Feminist scholarship is most certainly not a homogenous body of knowledge and there is a wide range of feminist theories that vary considerably depending on discipline and historical context (for an overview see Maclaran and Kravets, 2018). As some become dated and go out of fashion (e.g. standpoint feminism), others evolve (e.g. liberal feminism to neoliberal feminism), with new perspectives emerging (e.g. intersectional feminism). Whereas Marxist and socialist feminism has tended to dominate certain social sciences, when feminist scholarship emerged in marketing it was more focused on poststructuralist perspectives that prevailed in the humanities at the time. This was because of feminism in marketing's alignment with the burgeoning interpretivist movement of the 1990s that drew strongly on art, and the humanities more generally, for insights into consumers' lifeworlds. Poststructuralist theorising has also dominated much of Critical Management Studies critiques of organisations, particularly in terms of identifying power relations and exposing inequalities in organisational life. So it's worth taking a closer look at the insights (and, of course, the oversights!) that this theoretical position brings and its evolution within marketing.

POSTSTRUCTURALIST FEMINISM IN MARKETING

Poststructuralist thinking emerged in the 1960s with thinkers such as Foucault and Derrida who questioned established ways of knowledge creation and, indeed, the very idea of what counts as knowledge. An important focus of poststructuralism is who gets to decide something counts as knowledge or not because this exposes underlying power relations. As a mode of thinking, poststructuralism emphasises how discourse constitutes our reality and how meaning is constantly in flux, dependent on how something is constructed in a specific discursive field.[2] For example, a lightning bolt can be understood in geological terms as a natural phenomenon shaping mountains, whereas it may be interpreted as the act of a wrathful god in theological terms. Thus meanings shift and evolve over time and are dependent on cultural context. Poststructuralism's task is to deconstruct how specific discourses bear ideological assumptions that reflect a particular group's worldview and exclude other ways of understanding the world. On account of the dominance of patriarchal worldviews in most discursive fields, a dominance that is usually to the detriment of women, poststructuralist critique informs much feminist critique.

For poststructuralist feminists, gender is constructed in discourse. Categories such as male/female must therefore be understood in their historical and social contexts, as well as how one category is constructed in opposition to the other with one term usually privileged over the other. The principle of binary oppositions is fundamental to poststructuralist deconstruction because it makes visible how males become associated with the more valued category in any dualism and women with the lesser valued, for example mind/body, reason/emotion, culture/nature, active/ passive and so forth. These binaries are in constant dialogue and although this relationship changes with a particular socio-historic context, the more privileged term takes its meaning from not being its 'other'. Hence to be masculine is to deny any semblance of being feminine, namely, appearing soft, emotional, unassertive, and so forth. Moreover, because what is defined as masculine or feminine varies according to socio-historic context (particularly in relation to social class, ethnicity, religion and national or regional culture), there are many different forms of masculinity and femininity that interact in complex ways. For example, Mats Alvesson, a leading critical management scholar, conducted an ethnography of a Swedish advertising agency where he noted a strong gender division of labour, with men holding all the top hierarchical positions (Alvesson, 1998). Initially the replication of traditional gender norms puzzled him because advertising expertise is usually understood as privileging feminine values such as intuition, emotions and close friendships. Alvesson found, however, that the men's occupational identity – especially their feminised position in relation to the clients they handled – caused deep insecurities, resulting in the need to strengthen their sense of masculinity. Consequently, males in the agency enforced a strict gender division of labour with men at the top and women relegated to lower positions.

In a similar vein, early feminist critiques in marketing and consumer research applied feminist poststructuralist enquiry to reveal how much marketing thought is gendered. Marketing's rhetoric of exchange parallels discourse surrounding male/female relationships with power dynamics of seduction and submission, according to Fischer and Bristor (1994). A masculinist worldview, with its concomitant ideology of conflict and competition, means that marketing thought is replete with metaphors of war and combat: targeting and penetrating market segments; winning market share; and beating competitors (Hirschman, 1993). A 'man as computer' machine metaphor dominates consumer decision-making models that privilege mind over body and overlook the significance of embodied experiences (Joy and Venkatesh, 1994). The natural environment suffers acutely in the hands of this androcentric perspective that conceives of nature as merely a free resource to be (ab)used in pursuit of market development and profit motives (Dobscha, 1993).

Later marketing and consumer gender studies have been heavily influenced by the work of Judith Butler who is probably the best-known poststructuralist gender theorist. Her work has brought insights in relation to new masculinities (Schroeder and Zwick, 2004; Brownlie and Hewer, 2007) and performative femininities (Martin, Schouten and McAlexander, 2006;; Zayer et al., 2012; Stevens, Cappellini and Smith, 2015).

Butler's theory of gender performativity – elaborated in *Gender Trouble* (1990) and *Bodies that Matter* (1993) – identified the fluid nature of gender and sexuality with gender being something we 'do', rather than 'have'. In other words, gender is not fixed or stable, instead it is performed over and over again by words and actions whenever specific cultural repertoires are repeated (i.e. women baking in the kitchen, men doing DIY in the garden shed). Conceptualising gender as 'an ongoing discursive practice', Butler envisages the potential for disruption of this pattern through what she refers to as 'resignifications' (Butler, 1990, p. 33), an intervention whereby the ongoing iteration of norms are changed or challenged in some way. For example, Thompson and Üstüner (2015) illustrate how women's flat track roller derby can be viewed as disruptive in so far as normative ideals of femininity are juxtaposed against physical aggression and displays of playful eroticism. They are therefore a good example of resignification and even 'ideological edgework' that attempts to navigate wider social structures, and in doing so expand 'the discursive and material limits of gender performativity' (p. 257). Similarly, Harju and Huovinen's (2015) study of plus-size fashion bloggers reveals their destigmatisation of fat through subversive repetition of normative femininity for their own ends.

More often, though, women – and others perceived not to conform to gender norms such as the LGBTQI+ community – remain trapped within the constraints of gendered cultural repertoires. These dominate in many countries around the globe where patriarchal traditions are still tightly enforced and where these may even be used to condone extreme brutality (Joy, Belk and Bhardwaj, 2015). Butler's theories have exposed how a discourse of respectable consumption in India contributes to the normalisation of sexual violence against women. The androcentric discourse of *izzat* (respect or social honour) frames women as guardians of family traditions and positions the norms of consumption within this discourse (Varman, Goswami and Vijay, 2018). Consequently, any women perceived as deviating from these norms, but particularly those from lower castes and income, are demonised as unrespectable and dishonorable, held to blame for any violence that befalls them (e.g. rape and honour killings).

As our discussions show, poststructuralist thinking still carries relevance for current scholarship and its influence certainly continues to underpin contemporary theorisations on gender. Critiques have accused this body of thought of being too focused on discourse, however, stressing in particular how it overlooks crucial material realities. Although Butler's work addresses this oversight up to a point (especially her later work on precarity and precariousness that introduces a 'bodily ontology' – see Butler, 2004) other feminist theories, like Karen Barad's (2003) material-discursive approach, have contributed further to our understanding of lived experience and economic deprivation (see Steinfield, 2021).

TAKING GENDER RESEARCH FORWARD: THREE LEVELS OF UNDERSTANDING

In providing this brief overview of extant literature as a foundation for the chapters that follow, we find it useful to think of three distinct levels of conceptually understanding gender: the *socio-economic*, the *embodied-affective*, and the *representational* (see Chatzidakis and Maclaran, 2020). Of course, these levels are also interrelated and like any categorisation need to be treated cautiously but they do at least point to differing emphases in various bodies of scholarship. Let's now take a closer look at each of these categories as a way to highlight the work of influential gender theorists and discuss relevant contributions within marketing and consumer research.

Socio-Economic Understandings of Gender

One of the feminist literature's principal foci is the gender dimension of socio-economic injustices and the fact that many women do not have ready access to marketplace resources. Theorists like Angela McRobbie and Beverley Skeggs have been vociferous in arguing that the invitation to consume is not extended to all women (and neither is it to all genders), independent of means and status. Skeggs (1997) broke new ground in her book, *Formations of Class and Gender: Becoming Respectable*, where she charged feminist and cultural theorists with abandoning the intersection of gender and class. Such a socio-economic oversight, she claimed, detracted from issues of exploitation. Whose experiences are being silenced and why are they being overlooked? With these penetrating questions foregrounded in her work, Skeggs' ethnography of white working-class women revealed how class position blocks access to the economic, social, political and symbolic capitals required to attain 'respectability', a construct Skeggs uses as an analytic tool. In a similar vein, McRobbie (1997) exposed the British fashion industry for its unethical working conditions and production processes that exploit cheap female labour. She highlights how male-dominated management hierarchies in these factories often exacerbate gender inequities. Choices for women factory workers, like other working-class women Skeggs studies, are severely constrained by their economic circumstances and the prevailing patriarchal power dynamics.

Another leading feminist scholar, American critical theorist Nancy Fraser, usefully differentiates between politics of (economic) distribution versus those of (cultural) recognition (Fraser, 2013). Although both are closely interwoven in daily life, this analytic distinction helps us understand the different forms of political-economic and cultural-symbolic restructuring that each requires. There have been various critiques of Fraser's position (see, for example, Fraser and Honneth, 2003), including Judith Butler's contention that distribution and recognition are so closely interrelated that they cannot be effectively separated. Worthy of note here, however, is that Fraser's historical perspective reveals how the politics of recognition have been decoupled from the politics of redistribution in late capitalist societies. This point is especially relevant to our earlier comment about feminist consumer and marketing research becoming muted in the 1990s. At that time, the main emphasis in this body of research was on recognition rather than redistribution. It was therefore easy for gender scholarship to be seamlessly subsumed into broader postmodern and interpretivist gender identity debates. Of course, there are exceptions as we discuss below.

Linda Scott – Professor Emeritus at the Saïd Business School, Oxford University and founder of the Global Business Coalition for Women's Economic Empowerment (GBCWEE)[3] – has been a leading voice (and a somewhat lone one in marketing and consumer research until recently!) in the redistribution of economic resources to empower women in developing countries. Her work continues to emphasise the global societal benefits of closing the gender gap, namely: expanding national productivity; improved nutrition and overall health rates; and reduced child mortality (Scott et al., 2012). In defiance of what Scott sees as a dominant anti-capitalist attitude typifying much feminist discourse, she and her colleagues propose pragmatist feminism. This perspective is a syncretisation of classical American pragmatism – a philosophical position that recognises the importance of practical consequences rather than the production of abstract principles – and feminism. In keeping with this orientation, pragmatist feminism is not ideologically bound, but focuses instead on achievable outcomes and whatever means are available to realise these. Long a proponent of 'market feminism' (Scott, 2005), Scott and colleagues point to nation-level data from the World Economic Forum and the United Nations that highlights how women have the best conditions where global capitalism is most established. To this end Scott and her colleagues advocate re-examining history to evaluate what specific market conditions favour women's advancement and identify 'replicable innovations' that may lead to women's empowerment. Applying this approach to assessing Avon networks in South Africa with a large-scale multi-method research programme exploring the lifeworlds of Avon representatives there, Scott and her team conclude this avenue does indeed provide emancipatory opportunities for women and enable them to overcome infrastructural barriers. The caveat, as they stress, is that network marketing of this nature is not a one-size-fits-all solution to escaping poverty: the model needs to be adapted to local cultural and patriarchal mores.

More recent work in marketing and consumer research has built on this research, likewise trying to move the conversation beyond deception/authenticity debates that recur around corporate sponsorship of Women's Economic Empowerment (WEE) and polarise opinions needlessly. Taking a material discursive feminist approach (see Barad, 2003), Steinfield (2021) unpacks the various human/non-human entanglements that transpire over time in the marketisation and measurement of WEE efforts. Her longtitudinal case study of Walmart's WEE programme reveals the many interactions, metrics and marketing activities that combine to make certain aspects more (in)visible than others, including the role that academics can unintentionally play. For example, although Walmart's marketing of the programme positioned women as caregivers in publicity materials, the actual implementation of the programmes did little to facilitate an adequate work/life balance. Consequently, high-growth empowerment models allowed no space for women to juggle their family commitments. To this end, Steinfield (2021, p. 25) calls for a reality check that acknowledges specific contextual factors and recommends such programmes are co-created with the communities they are intended to help. She underlines the 'need for practitioners to realign the things of the marketing and marketisation of WEE so that they are more in line with a woman's reality, and to think more broadly about what needs to change (e.g. troubling gender norms/roles)'.

This body of feminist scholarship in marketing and consumer research is advancing our knowledge of the way power is (re)produced through marketing systems as well as how power flows relate to gender injustice. The complex mix of socio-economic factors, discursive practices and material realities in which these power relations are embedded is encapsulated in Hein et al.'s (2016) 'transformative gender justice framework' (TGJF) which they later put to the test in relation to the reproductive health market in Uganda (Steinfield et al., 2019). Above all, this framework reconciles distributive justice with recognition theory to offer a multi-paradigmatic lens that encourages a dialogic approach to global gender injustices on the part of policy makers, scholars and practitioners.

In summary then, socio-economic analyses of gender in marketing have been relatively few until recently. Now a dynamic group of feminist scholars, working from macromarketing and transformative consumer research perspectives, has offered more penetrating critiques of marketing's role in global inequalities, as well as pinpointing potential for positive interventions. There is much more work needed in this area and new avenues are continuously being opened up as more scholars pursue this important vein of research and build its momentum.

Embodied-Affective Understandings of Gender

In contrast to socio-economic perspectives that take as their primary focus the intersection of gender with economic and social injustices, much feminist theory stresses the inherently affective and embodied elements of gender, the taken-for-granted aspects that we assume are just 'normal' and outside the conventional realm of justice.

Theories of embodiment that bring the body and mind together have been central to feminist thinking. Notably, these theories revalidate the body, relegated to second place in Cartesian dualistic thinking that privileges mind (masculine) over body (feminine) – French philosopher, Rene Descartes' central tenet being 'I think therefore I am.' As Grosz (1994, p. 14) highlights, women are perceived to be 'somehow *more* biological, *more* corporeal, and *more* natural than men' and this enmeshment in bodily experience means they are likely to be seen as more fickle or emotional in their judgements in comparison to their male counterparts. Thus, for feminist thinkers like Elizabeth Grosz and Rosi Braidotti, embodiment of the subject must reconcile the mind/body split by bringing together the physical, the symbolic and the sociological (Braidotti, 1994). Such reconciliation means engaging with the relationships between representations of the body and actual embodied experiences – including social practices – across socio-cultural and historical contexts (Davis, 1997). A crucial part of this is overturning the many assumptions made about women's bodies that run deep through historical, political, social and cultural justifications for women's inferior status (Grosz, 1994). In her book, *Unbearable Weight*, Susan Bordo (1993) powerfully deconstructs the mind–body dualism – and its negativity associated with women – showing how its gendered ideology is profoundly embedded in all aspects of our lives from law and medicine, through literary and artistic representations to popular culture and advertising.

Analyses of embodiment are, therefore, essential to understanding how power relations govern sexual relations. In her book, *Volatile Bodies: Towards a Corporeal Feminism*, Grosz (1994) elucidates the role of bodily fluids in determining sexual difference. Many socio-cultural and historical contexts view women's bodies as a source of pollution and contamination for men. The reverse logic does not apply and men's bodies are seen as more self-contained than their female counterparts, with less risk of uncontrolled seepage or hysteria. Much feminist scholarship has built on Grosz's and Bordo's work to overturn these modernist and, ultimately, unfair patriarchal assumptions. Specifically within consumer research, feminist theories of embodiment and affectivity have helped us understand more about object–person relations, while also refuting the mind/body dichotomy. In their study of sleep culture and the gendered interactions consumers have with their beds, Valtonen and Närvänen (2015, p. 1595) conclude that while asleep '*both* male and female bodies are uncontrollable, irrational, disruptive and vulnerable. *Both* male and female bodies are also fluid, leaky and open – and partly outside will and intention.'

Theories of the body are also central to the work of French feminists like Hélène Cixous, Luce Irigaray and Julia Kristeva and their notion of 'écriture féminine'. Referring to the phallocentricism dominating literature and philosophy, they argued that 'writing for the body' could be used as a means of subversion. Drawing on psychoanalytic approaches they critiqued Freud's and Lacan's theories of femininity as being overly deterministic, phallocentric and one-dimensional. They used the concept of 'jouissance' to express women's creative power and pleasure (both physical and spiritual) as a way for women to express their own voices. In consumer research this notion, together with Irigaray's (1985) theory of female voyeurism – as detailed in *Speculum of the Other Woman* – has brought insights into the private world of women's magazine consumption (Stevens and Maclaran, 2000). For Irigaray, man is defined as subject and woman is defined as object with the man actively controlling the gaze (the voyeur) of which woman is the passive receptor. Irigaray uses her idea of the speculum to show how women can challenge this subject–object dualism by moving into the agentic position of the voyeuse, taking a journey into female self-hood that escapes the male gaze. By providing a sense of community and identification with other women, magazine reading can facilitate this introspective process. In learning about other women's experiences, women learned more about themselves, taking back the gaze and thereby reinstating themselves as the subject rather than the object of this.

Kristeva's (1982) concept of abjection – the feelings of horror an individual experiences when faced with a corporeal reality such as leaky bodies, slime or even death – has helped reveal how anthropomorphised images of cows in advertising (e.g. Elsie the Borden Cow) conceal androcentric attitudes and embedded cultural biases (Stevens, Maclaran and Kearney, 2014). Abjection also helps explain negative consequences of consumer experience in the Dans le Noir restaurant chain where diners eat in the pitch dark and are served by blind staff. For Kristeva, subjecthood depends on being constantly vigilant to the abject. We are constantly trying to exclude anything perceived as abject because of the loss of distinction it implies between subject and object, between self and others. This ambiguity threatens us with a complete breakdown in meaning. Hence, although the restaurant chain claims the Dans le Noir experience builds empathy between customers and staff, in fact its servicescape manufactures processes of abjection whereby blind waiters, and the very concept of blindness itself, are discursively inscribed within the consumer experience (Davies, Maclaran and Tissiers-Desbordes, 2015). Empathy is perverted by the powers of horror with the overall effect of evoking sympathy instead that reasserts boundaries of the self as not-blind and 'othering' those who are blind.

Drawing further on psychoanalysis and poststructuralism, we return once again to Judith Butler. Her concept of *heteronormativity* is particularly enlightening for embodied-affective understandings of gender and helps reconcile some of the critiques of essentialism levelled at the French feminist thinkers. Unlike many feminists who distinguish between sex (a biological category) and gender (a social construction), Butler sees both sex and gender as socially constructed and brings these together in what she termed 'the heteronormative matrix'. Heternormativity refers to the apparent natural correspondence between binary categories of sex, gender and desire. In turn, these relate to Butler's notion of gender *performativity*, to which we referred earlier: the idea that gender is always a doing and constitutive of the very identity it supposedly performs. As we already demonstrated, markets and consumption practices can therefore either reinforce these gender norms by reproducing them in ways that go unquestioned or they can subvert them by refusing to adhere to them. Within the context of LGBTQI+ festivals, for instance, acts of excessive, dramatised and overly sexualised consumption symbolically invert the marginalisation of everyday gender-atypical consumption. In addition, the extent of shopping and commercialisation witnessed during the festival on the whole serves to express the purchasing and political power of the LGBTQI+ population.

However, deviation from a norm does not necessarily equate to subversion, particularly when most norms depend on a certain percentage of deviant cases for their survival (Foucault, 1977). In other words, gender-atypical consumption may be used as a means of self-affirmation or identity revaluation without destabilising heteronormativity, doing little to challenge entrenched social hierarchies and power relations in the longer term. Hence, although the flamboyant consumption acts during LGBTQI+ festivals may serve in the short term to affirm a gay identity, if dissociated from the everyday norms of heteronormative consumption, they do little to challenge any of the binary categories that make gendered consumption intelligible.

A final strand of feminist research relevant to this section concerns the field of consumer ethics within marketing and focuses on the affective aspects of gendered thinking and decision-making. The focus here is enlightenment ideals of the seemingly autonomous and rational moral subject (that is always a man), ideals that are largely incompatible with feminine traits and modes of reasoning. Accordingly, 'care ethics' scholars such as Carol Gilligan (1982), Joan Tronto (1993) and Nel Noddings (2003), have foregrounded a different type of reasoning that is (understood as) more feminine in its embracement of relationality, interdependency and empathy. For care ethics scholars, consumers (and marketers) face multiple caring demands and dilemmas that cannot be disembedded from the rich context of their everyday experiences. It is also important to emphasise that caring is viewed as fundamentally gendered (e.g. Noddings, 2003) because, historically, it has been restricted within the domain of private household activity as opposed to the public polis; with women bearing the burden of caring responsibilities and men being free to participate in more 'serious' political affairs. Gilligan

(1982) famously extends the critique of moral reasoning by pointing to how Kohlberg's (1969) influential model of children's moral development was based on interviews with males, and therefore was inevitably biased in favour of highly masculine values (e.g. abstract and impartial reasoning) as opposed to feminine ones (e.g. interdependency, care and affective reasoning).

Building on this tradition, consumer researchers have recently begun departing from largely de-contextualised and abstract models of ethical decision-making, such as Ajzen's (1991) attitudinal Theory of Planned Behaviour and Hunt and Vitell's (1986) general theory of marketing ethics; and to re-conceptualise consumers' moral choices as matters of care and caring dilemmas (e.g. Heath et al., 2016; Shaw et al., 2016). Indeed, the inherent 'masculinity' bias in these models has to be redressed through the development of accounts that acknowledge not only the affective and embodied dimensions of everyday consumption but also its inherently social and interdependent nature. Within anthropology, for instance, it has long been asserted that ordinary shopping is not as atomised and individualist as colloquial understandings would suggest. Rather, it is commonly done with others in mind and is deeply embedded in norms and rituals of care, empathy and love for others (Miller, 1998). This observation is echoed within the more activist-oriented literature, whereby the language of care and interdependence is seen as essential to the development of more genuinely progressive research and activist agendas (e.g. Littler, 2009).

Representation and Gender

Finally, gender is constructed and reproduced continually via media consumption. Our gendered norms and values are profoundly and fundamentally influenced by the various media representations of different genders across advertising, branding, journalism, TV and popular music. Existing stereotypes are both constitutive of and constituted by these representations. Furthermore, by rendering visible some gendered identities and invisibilising others, the media also under- and/or misrepresents particular identity positions, ultimately enabling their marginalisation and stigmatisation. An early critic of media representations has been feminist writer, Betty Friedan. In her seminal book, *The Feminine Mystique* (1963), Friedan exposed the hypocrisy behind popular representations of the contented housewife, successfully tending to the needs of her family while happily managing her natural domain, the private domestic sphere.

Friedan astutely showed how the gendered binary of public versus private spheres (also mentioned above) served to reinforce a patriarchal ideology that undervalued and under-resourced domesticity. This split ensured women took charge of the domestic sphere while men happily embraced their participation in the more valuable, public sphere. Building on this tradition but coming from a visual studies perspective, feminist film theorist Laura Mulvey introduced the notion of the 'male gaze', a term that conveys how the visual language of films is designed to empower the male viewer whilst sexualising and objectifying women (Mulvey, 1975). Mulvey's work asserts that masculine voyeurism dominates cinematic representations, with women adopting the role of the spectacle and men the role of the spectator (Stevens and Maclaran, 2000). Corroborating Mulvey's insights and adding a more psychoanalytic perspective, Luce Irigaray (1985) exposes the masculine nature of interests and values that are encoded into the presumably non-sexualised subject of Western discourse. Echoing de Beauvoir (1949), Irigaray notes how women are naturalised as the other and/or with nature, as opposed to being a subject in their own right.

Advertising research responded to such criticisms from the 1970s onwards, focusing on female portrayals and the extent to which they evolved in tandem with their changing societal roles (Wagner and Banos, 1973; Sexton and Haberman, 1974; Belkaoui and Belkaoui, 1976). Often adopting a more managerial and profit-driven agenda, some of these studies explored how stereotyping influenced women's self-image and in turn, their intentions to buy specific services and products. For example, more progressive, professionally orientated role portrayals were deemed as more effective in promoting beauty products and other self-image-oriented products, whereas more traditional role portrayals were still deemed as more suitable for the promotion of products such as household goods (Courtney and Whipple, 1983). The majority of this work remained descriptive and rather uncritical until the 1990s when, influenced by postmodern and social constructivist perspectives, interpretivist consumer researchers helped to expose the implicit power relations that were inherent to stereotypical gender representations (Stern and Holbrook, 1994). Among others, feminist consumer researchers criticised the machine metaphor that underlined dominant conceptualisations of the consumer buying process. These privileged the economic, rational actor (homo economicus) that engaged in impartial cognitive information processing (the mind understood as masculine), rather than more embodied and affective dimensions underpinning most consumption activity (the body understood as feminine).

Thanks to sustained feminist critiques of advertising, from the 1980s onwards, advertisers began to create more female empowering images and messages and to develop more varied representations of masculinity in their attempt to better segment and target male consumers (Mort, 2013). Concurrently, consumer researchers expanded their focus to include topics such as the shifting range of masculinities manifest in the media – from the man-of-action-hero (Holt and Thompson, 2004) to more domestic portrayals (Moisio, Arnould and Gentry, 2013; Marshall et al., 2014) to the advent of the metrosexual (Rinallo, 2007). Such studies also increasingly recognised men's vulnerability as a result of having to live up to unrealistic gender ideals (i.e. hegemonic masculinity) and how such representations of masculinity could be just as damaging to men as those of femininity to women (Patterson and Elliott, 2002; Zayer and Otnes, 2012).

Paralleling such developments, other studies focused on media representations of LGBTQI+ and gender nonconforming men and women (Borgerson et al., 2006; Tsai, 2010) and how these can be profoundly repressive and damaging; not least from a heteronormative perspective that silences both non-normative sexualities and the blurring or bending of genders as in the case of non-binary, transgender or transsexual individuals. Despite the increasing social awareness of transgender issues, for instance, this group is still exposed to heightened vulnerability and stigmatisation with little positive or non-normative representation in the media (Rowe and Rowe, 2015). One potential example in the right direction is the representation of the transgendered Ms Hudson in the US television series, *Elementary*, a contemporary version of the Sherlock Holmes story. Ms Hudson's trangender status is not a central part of narrative, rather the protagonist is simply accepted as such, and played by the transgendered actress, Candis Cayne. By not re-emphasising or letting the narrative evolve around the protagonist's gender identity, the programme avoids assessing it against heteronormative standards: her gendered positioning does not need to be questioned or explained and that's the point (Maclaran and Otnes, 2017).

In sum, the wealth of prior research on gender and marketing is testament to the critical role that marketplace actors play, in their various roles (from advertisers and social media experts to retailers and mass media funders), in the reproduction of gender norms and stereotypes, as well as the marginalisation and invisibilisation of gender nonconforming individuals. This also highlights the need for more collective and institutional responses that move beyond the individual consumer and their buying behaviour. A more multi-stakeholder approach would emphasise, for instance, the need for consumer groups and organisations (e.g. ethicalconsumer.org) to lobby government or liaise with regulatory bodies to achieve change.

STRUCTURE OF THE BOOK

With this brief overview of prominent feminist theories and our summary of the field to date we hope to have paved the way for the chapters that follow and we will return to many of the themes we have raised to develop and deepen them. Our next chapter concerns the silences in marketing and consumer research. The marketing canon is almost exclusively male (see, for example, Sage's *Legends in Marketing and Consumer Research*). Chapter 2 considers voices that are absent from the canon, particularly the work of the early home economists and the women who worked in advertising agencies (see Zuckerman and Carsky, 1992; Tadajewski and Maclaran, 2013; Davis, 2016). It also introduces certain women entrepreneurs who made distinct contributions to marketing strategy and practice.

Advertising and, more generally, marketing communications are the focus of Chapter 3. Marketing communications have had a very bad press over the years for their role in reinforcing passive, decorative images of women. Emphasising theories of the 'male gaze' and Butler's concept of performativity (Butler, 1990), this chapter reviews the gendered nature of many marketing messages and campaigns, looking at how empowerment is now the leitmotif of appeals to women. We question the effectiveness of this through the lens of neoliberal feminism, while acknowledging that positive images of gender diversity may lead to changing social perceptions despite the current tendency to 'wokewash'.

The very development of markets can be gendered (consider Marlboro cigarettes that initially targeted female consumers, only to later reposition the brand as masculine, using the infamous rugged and macho Marlboro cowboy), so Chapter 4 takes a look at product and service innovations, in tandem with considering the intersection of new technologies and marketing, both offline and online. Technology is an especially gendered field and unequal gender relations shape its design and development. This carries over to the online environment where a misogynistic culture in male-dominated internet communities flourishes alongside the pornification of culture.

Over-consumption, plastics pollution, squandering the earth's natural but finite resources – so many negatives associated with markets and marketing activities imply environmental damage and destruction. Using ecofeminism as a lens, Chapter 5 examines how most marketing thought and action is rooted in the dominant social paradigm, a paradigm that is inherently androcentric and lacking in concern for the anthropocene (Kilbourne, 2004). From this perspective, caring for the environment is 'women's work' and, as such, devalued. Indeed, care itself is another free externality that to date has been overlooked, as this chapter goes on to illustrate.

Chapter 6 turns to marketing's internalities, exploring its organisational aspects and how these can be gendered. Women in marketing are most likely to be in some type of customer-facing role, whereas their male colleagues are to be found in more strategic marketing roles that are often higher-ranking, better paid and more likely to be at board level (Maclaran, Catterall and Stevens, 1997). Women are stereotypically seen as being appropriate for the caring aspects of the organisation. In many ways, little seems to have changed over the last 20 years. Although there are many more women than men in marketing associate positions (two-thirds female to one-third male),[4] there continues to be many more men in senior positions (one-third female to two-thirds male). We also contemplate the question of whether the marketing organisation can really be caring as we engage with a notion of care that is more central to feminist ethics, a notion that requires deeper involvement with a wider array of relationships inside and outside the organisation.

Where do all these analyses lead us? In Chapter 7 we envision ways for marketing and markets to have a more positive and progessive egalitarian influence on both practitioners and consumers. Exploring future possibilities in terms of theory and practice for how markets and marketing activities can contribute, we engage with notions of demarketing and de-gendering marketing logics. As we do so, we also highlight newer feminist theories with potential to offer insightful new directions and lead the discipline forward.

NOTES

1. The red pill refers to a scene in 1999 film *The Matrix* when Keanu Reeve's character is offered a choice of a blue pill to remain in blissful ignorance or a red pill that will free the mind and let you know your enemy.
2. This is a concept originated by Foucault. Weedon (1987, p. 34) defines discursive fields as consisting of 'competing ways of giving meaning to the world and of organizing social institutions and processes'.
3. GBCWEE comprises a group of nine multi-national corporations – Coca-Cola, ExxonMobil, Goldman Sachs, Walmart, Marks & Spencer, Mastercard, Qualcomm, PwC, and Mondelez – dedicated to developing practices that support gender equality in the world economy.
4. https://careersmart.org.uk/occupations/marketing-and-sales-directors   and https://careersmart.org.uk/occupations/equality/which-jobs-do-men-and -women-do-occupational-breakdown-gender

2. Breaking the silences: women in the history of marketing thought and practice

Contemporary popular culture is replete with biographical dramas about women that history forgot. Viewers avidly consume films like *Colette* (2018), *The Wife* (2017) and *Mary Shelley* (2017) depicting the stories of brilliant female writers who are overshadowed by their less talented, but more celebrated, husbands. *Hidden Figures* (2016) foregrounds the role of three African American female mathematicians – known as human computers on account of their amazing calculating abilities – in the space race and the biases they faced as they rose through the ranks of NASA. In addition, a biting exposé of the gender gap in a world built by men, for men, *Invisible Women* by feminist activist and journalist Caroline Criado Perez, has received widespread acclaim after winning the Royal Society Science book award. Revealing how everything from office temperature controls to bullet-proof vests are designed with the male form as the default body, Criado Perez (2019) evokes the gender data gap that historically pervades research and effects policy decisions to the detriment of women's lives.

The evident thirst for women's history reflects a pressing priority for feminist scholars: the investigation into how specific bodies of knowledge are gendered and how women's voices – be they articulations of their feelings and experiences or their inputs in terms of ideas and insights – are missing from historical accounts. Two key goals are: (1) to counter the exclusion of women from history; and (2) to redress the negative characterisation of women (or the feminine) therein. Feminist epistemology seeks to redress women's sense of alienation; the fact that what women read often does not resonate with their own reality. Because historically women have not participated in the production of disciplinary knowledge, there are vast silences from half the population. No matter which discipline we consider – across the social and physical sciences as well as the humanities – women's voices are an absent presence.

In the previous chapter we highlighted the gendering of marketing knowledge in relation to its rhetorics (Hirschman, 1993; Fischer and Bristor, 1994) Now, in relation to the twin goals of feminist history, we go deeper into the silences that business history and marketing thought contain, as well as foregrounding the many significant contributions that women have made to both theory and practice.

GENDERING BUSINESS HISTORY

There is a tendency to presume that because few women are profiled or mentioned in the various histories of business they were not present in sufficient numbers or their contributions were minimal or irrelevant. The history of business is itself a gendered enterprise, however, and we need to take care in making such assumptions (Gamber, 1998; Lewis, 2009). Let's not forget that a prized resource for business historians is the corporate archive, usually seen as a masculine endeavour that mainly contains male voices (Durepos, McKinlay and Taylor, 2017). Wendy Gamber, in her analysis of small business in the 19th century, illustrates the tens of thousands of American women running small businesses at the time and how they were not acknowledged in the mainstream either at the time or in later histories. These female entrepreneurs were to be found in a range of successful small enterprises covering feminine finery (dressmakers, milliners, jewellers), boarding houses, grocery shops, bookstores, apothecaries, midwives, fortune-tellers and even brothel keepers. Gamber estimates that female-owned businesses represented one-tenth of urban business people in the mid-1800s. Through her investigations of credit reports from mid-19th-century Albany City in New York State, Lewis (2009) discovered more than 400 women-owned businesses. Yet, the stories of female entrepreneurs from this period remain largely untold.

One reason for the silence around women-owned business is the presumption by business historians that the entrepreneurial figure is a man, a notion that continues even today. Schumpeter's (1934) conception of the modern entrepreneur equivocates to the warrior in ancient society, a symbol of heroic masculinity emphasising a combative, conquering model of the entrepreneur (Kravets, Preece and Maclaran, 2020). This model remains pervasive in popular culture and brand mythology with entrepreneurial figures like Steve Jobs and Steve Wozniak, positioned as charismatic, visionary individuals who challenge mainstream corporate conglomerates such as IBM and Microsoft. Jones (2014, p. 240) has highlighted how such discourse creates a 'fictive entrepreneur', providing a norm against which female and ethnic minority entrepreneurs are often found wanting because they are not male or white. In addition, the ubiquitous Western notion of the self-made man reinforces an entrepreneurial stereotype as one who takes risks, is independent and in control (Hanson, 2003; Hovorka and Dietrich, 2011). These biases are encoded in research designs as Ahl's (2006) study of 81 academic articles on women's entrepreneurship revealed. Measurement scales used words associated with maleness to correspond with entrepreneurship and those associated with femaleness to indicate shortcomings. Consequently, the female entrepreneur is seen as something of an oxymoron, 'othered' in terms of definitions that delineate masculine traits as the default entrepreneur.

Biases such as these are then carried through to many historical analyses that do not associate female business owners with the risk-taking propensities assumed to be at the heart of entrepreneurship. Furthermore, as Gamber (1998) highlights, often these small businesses were not considered sufficiently large to be counted in samples or their owners were excluded on account of being self-employed. Sometimes, too, they operated at the borders of public and private domains making it difficult to categorise them in terms of economic contributions.

Turning to other business disciplines, scholars have also begun to reinstate the role of women and question the gendered nature of their profession. Cooke (1999) shows how women's previously unacknowledged contributions are being written into the histories of organisation development. Black (2006) draws attention to the pioneering efforts of female accountants during the First World War, while Spruill and Wootton (1995) document the leading role of Jennie Palen (1891–1991) in gaining acceptance for women in public accounting and within major accounting firms (albeit that their roles were frequently restricted to tax affairs that did not involve too much travel or client contact!). Using historical data from PricewaterhouseCoopers, Evans and Rumens (2020) expose the gendered processes underpinning the early professionalisation of accountancy with the qualities to be considered a 'professional' synonymous with male practices and masculinity.

MARKETING AND CONSUMER RESEARCH LEGENDS[1]

Given the evident gendering of business history, it is scarcely surprising that as we turn to marketing and consumer research we find similar biases prevailing. Indeed, as we delve into the history of marketing, probably the only woman most of many of us are likely to have come across is Maria Parloa, an American author of books on cooking and housekeeping (1843–1909). Published in 1908, her book, *Miss Parloa's New Cook Book and Marketing Guide*, is an oft-cited example of the early use of the term 'marketing'. But when it comes to the history of marketing thought, women do not feature in the long list of male marketing scholars noted for their contributions to the discipline: Robert Bartels, Wroe Alderson, Paul Converse, Shelby Hunt, Philip Kotler to name but a few well-known figures. Two Sage Publications series, *Legends in Marketing* and *Legends in Consumer Behaviour* deem only male scholars to be 'legends'. The Wikipedia page on the history of marketing lists only one female scholar – Valerie Zeithami (known for her work on service quality) – in its section on early marketing theorists.

Have there really been no other major influential female thinkers in marketing and consumer research? A few notable women's names certainly spring to mind, such as Elizabeth Hirschman, Barbara Stern and Barbara Kahn. So key questions we must ask at this point are: whose past does the history of marketing thought represent; and are some voices being deemed more credible than others? To find answers, we need to explore more deeply whether certain voices have been ignored due to prevailing historical and socio-cultural factors. In other words, we need to examine marketing's historical hierarchies of knowledge production to recognise hidden and silenced knowledge that may be due to gender inequity. Nor does this silencing solely concern those who are deemed the marketing scholars worthy of recognition; silencing can also apply to the subjects of our research. Often the experiences of particular groups may be excluded from theorising and their voices never heard in our accounts of marketing. A good example here is that until fairly recently economically disadvantaged groups and people with disabilities did not have their lifeworlds represented (excepting the work of a handful of notable scholars, e.g. Downey, 2016; Hamilton, Dunnett and Piacentini, 2016). The silenced subjects of our research will be returned to later, but for now we try to recover voices missing from the marketing canon in terms of their contributions to both theory and practice. To advance this task we draw on the work of other marketing scholars such as Mary Zuckerman, Mary Carsky, Judy Foster Davis, Jennifer Scanlon, Liz Parsons and Mark Tadajewski who have already provided compelling accounts of women marketing scholars and practitioners. In addition, we provide some further examples of our own as we focus on four important groups of women: (1) home economists from the early half of the 20th century; (2) female practitioners who worked in advertising agencies; (3) women who played a major role in marketing and consumer research activism; and (4) female entrepreneurs who have excelled at marketing practice.

HOME ECONOMISTS AND THEIR CONTRIBUTIONS TO MARKETING THOUGHT

Like marketing, the discipline of Home Economics (HE) emerged in the early part of the 20th century. The aim of HE courses was to professionalise the work of women and they incorporated a variety of scientific disciplines into the classroom to achieve this. This new pathway enabled women to have a university education when many subject areas were off limits to them (Zuckerman and Carsky, 1990). It was also the route to a professorship for a very small number.

Significantly, home economists pioneered the study of consumption before the marketing discipline, as well as developing much consumer behaviour theory and their programmes often included marketing courses. They played significant roles in diffusing consumer culture, acting as a bridge between production and consumption, domesticity and industry. An example is how they diffused the use of electricity in the first half of the 20th century, by promoting the use of technology in the home and educating consumers on its use. Some home economists also played a pivotal role in the redevelopment and repositioning of iconic household products. Professor Lucy Maltby, for instance, is known for introducing a 'woman's perspective' in the design of the Pyrex line of bakeware, ultimately helping the company to align textures and sizes with the recipes and technological affordances of her era.[2]

Home economist Hazel Kyrk's seminal work, *A Theory of Consumption*, published in 1923, introduced many new ideas at the time. Primarily she critiqued the traditional economic view of consumption that ignored the many varied motivations and impulses of consumers (Parsons, 2013; Tadajewski, 2013). It was a mistake, Kyrk argued, to attribute 'utility maximisation' as an umbrella reason for all consumption and much more nuanced understandings were required. Fascinated by the human behaviours that consumption involved, she therefore drew from both sociology and anthropology to analyse the many different consumption patterns she witnessed. Central to her book were the questions of consumer welfare in a free-enterprise, mass-production society and, in her own words, the 'why' of consumers' desires and their relative intensity (Tadajewski,

2013). As such she had already begun to address many questions that the interpretivist research paradigm would introduce some 50 years later! In the following quote we can see how she places emphasis on the impending pleasures of consumption, thus foreshadowing Holbrook's and Hirschman's feelings, fantasies and fun in the 1980s:

> Value is the 'shadow which coming consumption throws before.' It comes from the anticipation of the 'enjoyment' or satisfaction which is consequent upon the utilization of the goods chosen. Choices represent the individual's attempt to secure this enjoyment or satisfaction, and it is this anticipated 'pleasure' or gratification which explains why goods are wanted. (Kyrk, 1923)

Like her fellow home economist Hazel Kyrk, Elizabeth Ellis Hoyt also drew on sociological and anthropological sources to inform her work. In her first book, *Primitive Trade: Its Psychology and Economics* (1926), she drew widely on anthropology covering a multitude of different trading practices around the world. But it was her two books on consumption economics – *The Consumption of Wealth* (1928) and *Consumption in Our Society* (1938) – that are most significant to marketing. Whereas prior to Kyrk and Hoyt economics had pretty much ignored the household, viewing it as outside the realm of rational analysis, Hoyt's books (like Kyrk's) demonstrated how economic theory was also relevant to the allocation of resources in the home (Parsons, 2013). She was especially interested in the intersection of culture with consumption and sought to better understand choice and why preferences vary from group to group, as well as how consumers come to attribute value to specific goods and services. In her work she moved well beyond traditional economic value-in-use perspective and looked at the influence of fashion, taste and aesthetics. In addition, Hoyt expanded the concept of consumption to involve time, energy and money, a view that is taken for granted today, but was highly innovative at the time (Parsons, 2013).

The last home economist we discuss here is Christine Frederick. Although a home economist by training, she became an advertising consultant and consumer advocate who also advised marketers on how to approach consumers. She was a well-known champion of scientific management principles for home efficiency. So in other words, while Frederick Winslow Taylor was applying engineering principles to managing the factory floor, she was redefining the home as a site of production, using similar principles. In practice, this meant standardising household tasks through labour-saving devices or breaking jobs into separate operations to maximise efficiency. In fact she is credited with standardising heights of kitchen counters and work surfaces, and she was widely acclaimed for her streamlined kitchen layouts that minimised unnecessary domestic labour (see Figure 2.1).

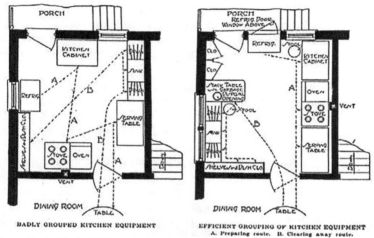

BADLY GROUPED KITCHEN EQUIPMENT

EFFICIENT GROUPING OF KITCHEN EQUIPMENT
A. Preparing route. B. Clearing away route.

Source: Frederick, C. (1923), *Household Engineering: Scientific Management in the Home*, Chicago: American School of Home Economics. Creative Commons Licence: Attribution-ShareAlike 4.0 International (CC BY-SA 4.0). https://creativecommons.org/licenses/by-sa/4.0/

Figure 2.1   Christine Frederick's efficiency kitchen design

Kitchen design apart, her major contribution to marketing knowledge was her 1929 book, *Selling Mrs Consumer*, a book intended for marketers and marketing educators in which she emphasised the importance of female consumers and detailed their differing consumer behaviours across a wide variety of product categories. Here she introduced original ideas such as the importance of selling healthy eating to consumers and the idea of 'progressive obsolescence', a term she used for the love of and willingness to pay for the new.

Her chapter on 'Obsolescence, Style and the American Consumer' rails against the presumption that the quest for the new is simply about 'keeping up with the Joneses', a traditional 'old school' European value that looks down on consumerism. In her words 'Mrs Consumer has called a halt. Our America is to be something better than a shoddy Europe.' She singles out English women, continuing, 'it is not uncommon for English Women of certain circles to wear on all formal occasions the same evening gown for 5 or 10 years. To us this is unheard of and preposterous!' In the same discussions she even refers to co-creation using this term to describe how American consumers have taken the modernistic trends out of the hands of Europeans and are now the 'co-creators' of it as opposed to the 'imitators'. Again she was way ahead of her time in emphasising a much more agentic model of value creation than presupposed by economic theory of the time.

Together these three vignettes capture some of the early insights on consumer behaviour made by home economists; insights that preceded marketing's scholarly interest in consumer research by several decades. It seems, however, that their early conceptualisations of the consumer were given little lasting attention – especially after marketing separated from economics as a discipline in the early 20th century. In addition, a growing gap between early home economists' aspirations and institutional pressures to provide vocational training, as well as sustained critique by feminists who saw the field as reinscribing essentialist understandings of womanhood and domesticity, led to the field's increasing lack of legitimacy and ultimate demise. The contributions of home economists are therefore all but forgotten and rarely cited in marketing and beyond. In 1992, Gary Becker – who had worked alongside Kyrk at the University of Chicago – received the Nobel prize for his work on the 'new household economics', work that had been pioneered by the home economists more than 50 years before.

WOMEN IN ADVERTISING AND THEIR CONTRIBUTIONS TO MARKETING PRACTICE

Women in advertising also had to face many structural barriers. In fact, the advertising industry has had historically low participation by both women and people of colour, biases that remain to the present day. Inspired by the emergence of the 'New Woman', towards the end of the 19th century women were beginning to enter the workplace in larger numbers. However, even if college educated, opportunities for women were limited to mainly clerical positions in the business world.

Nevertheless, as with home economics, opportunities opened in the advertising industry for 'female expertise' to advise on female consumers, even while such positions remained marginalised in terms of status through their associations with 'women's work'. For example in 1912 women who attended a meeting of the Advertising Men's League of New York were only allowed to be present on the balcony and behind a curtain. This led to the proliferation of women's advertising clubs that were colloquially referred to as Jane Martin's Sewing Circle (after the founder of the New York Women's League).

At this time J. Walter Thompson offered the best early opportunities for women copywriters in its Women's Editorial Department where they worked in a women's world, i.e. with other women, on products and ads targeting women. Women were kept well away from broader business functions such as finance with one company treasurer in 1922 arguing that women, 'while their initiatives are usually excellent, are lacking in basic ethical sense'.

This was the milieu in which Helen Lansdowne Resor – known as the most successful copywriter of her generation – found herself. Although she was married to JWT's co-president, Stanley Resor, she had established herself as an independent woman with a strong career profile before her marriage to Stanley. She ran the Women's Editorial Department at JWT where she helped establish equality for female employees, paying women copywriters the same as their male colleagues and encouraging their advancement through creative work (Scanlon, 2013).

It may come as a surprise to discover that a woman first introduced sex appeal into advertising, but this is credited to Helen with her strapline 'a skin you love to touch' – a strapline that created a huge controversy at the time. Her campaigns were marked out by their use of visual sensuality, and she developed various research techniques to underpin such campaigns (Scanlon, 2013). She was also an early pioneer in the use of advertorials to foster relationships between the consumer and product (see Figure 2.2).

This campaign created in 1916 is a good example of early lifestyle marketing on a mundane product. Scanlon's work reveals that when Lever brought LUX to JWT, Helen and her team were responsible for replacing its then well-worn tagline 'LUX won't shrink woollens' with 'LUX for all fine fabrics', transforming LUX into an aspirational brand and tapping into women's desires for a refinement that transcended their domesticity. The huge success of this campaign, along with their many other creative insights meant that by 1918, Helen Resor and her team accounted for over 50 per cent of the total agency revenue. They changed the face of advertising by integrating it into women's magazines, and by using state-of-the-art techniques to research and write ads.

Figure 2.2   Helen Resor's LUX campaign

Although Caroline Robinson Jones was born some 50+ years after Helen Resor, she still had to overcome many structural barriers to pursue her career in advertising in the 1960s. Anyone who has followed the TV series *Mad Men* will understand the rampant sexism and misogyny that dominated the advertising industry at that time. And if the industry was hard for women to enter, it was doubly so for women of colour, as Judy Foster Davis has so vividly illustrated in her book, *Pioneering African-American in the Advertising Business: Biographies of MAD black WOMEN* (2016). Yet, Caroline built her reputation as the leading African American woman in the advertising business. This is no small feat when we remember that Coca-Cola only introduced its first woman of colour in its ads during 1955, eight years before Caroline graduated from the University of Michigan in 1963. Despite her qualifications, she started at JWT as a secretary – the main opportunity for women to get employment at an ad agency until the 1970s. Caroline hoped that, once employed there, she would be well placed for one of the limited copy-writing jobs available. So impressive were her copywriting skills that she was able to transfer roles in a very short time to become the first black copywriter at JWT.

Incredibly, not much had changed since Helen Resor's time in relation to the gendered division of labour. Women copywriters were still assigned to women's products, a responsibility that meant they were taken less seriously and given less status. Jones found this deeply frustrating, particularly as she was expected to be expert only on African American consumers on account of her ethnicity. She championed the potential for a multi-ethnic approach to marketing, trying to get JWT to have ethnic models included in ads that were not just targeting black consumers and Hispanics (Davis, 2013). After all, she argued, the general population is a mixture of races and ethnicities, not just white Caucasian, and she believed this should be reflected in more national, mass marketing campaigns. When her advice was ignored, she became disillusioned with JWT and left the agency.

Caroline continued all her life to pioneer multi-ethnic marketing, as Davis (2013) documents in detail in tracking her career trajectory. Caroline's first move in this respect was as co-founder of Zebra Associates, one of the first African American ad agencies. Then, moving on from this venture, she later became the first African American vice president of a major advertising agency, BBDO (Batten, Barton, Durstine & Osborn), New York. Ultimately, she founded her own advertising agency, Caroline Jones Advertising. With high-profile clients such as American Express and Prudential, her reputation was on a national scale rather than regional or demographic specific. All her career she fought to have black advertising professionals recognised in their own right – as experts in media communications – and not just as 'experts' in relation to African American consumers. Awards that she received are further testimony to her professional recognition; she was voted Advertising Woman of the Year (1990) and featured in *The Wall Street Journal*'s series on 'Creative Leaders'. At that time she was the only black person to have received such accolades.

WOMEN ACTIVISTS IN MARKETING AND CONSUMER RESEARCH

Women are often (also) silenced in the history of marketing and consumer activism yet their role has been anything but peripheral, despite the difficulty in drawing clear historical linkages and genealogical connections between different modes and types of activism (see Newholm and Newholm, 2016). The infamous sugar boycotts of the late 18th and early 19th centuries, for instance, were primarily organised and performed by women.

Whereas men's role in anti-slavery activism has been far more documented and typically viewed as more significant, based as it was in the public sphere of the then British Empire, the women's boycotting movement of slave-produced products was unprecedented in terms of commitment and perseverance. Following the failure of the British Parliament to pass the Abolitionist Bill of 1789, there were nationwide calls for boycotting sugar produced in the West Indies. This, for women, represented a unique opportunity for political action at a pre-suffragette time when voting was viewed as the natural prerogative of men. At its peak, the so-called British boycott had more than 400,000 participants (mostly women) and resulted, in just over few months, in a drop in demand for West Indies sugar by at least a third and a parallel tenfold increase in demand for Indian sugar.[3] Although originally called for by William Fox in 1791, through a pamphlet that was hailed as the most popular pamphlet of the century, there is no doubt that the sugar boycott was primarily supported and executed by female anti-slavery associations that distributed further pamphlets and leaflets door to door. In the area of Birmingham, for instance, these included '[s]ystematic house-to-house canvasses ... with women visiting every house over a period of several years' (Midgley, 1996, p. 41).

During the second wave of the sugar boycott, circa the 1820s and largely in response to politicians' 'gradualist' as opposed to immediate abolition of the slave trade (despite its official abolition in 1808), prominent women such as Elisabeth Heyrick took centre stage, visiting shops all around Leicester and encouraging women to politicise their buying decisions. In a pamphlet entitled 'Appeal to the Hearts and Consciences of British Women', Heyrick (1828) encouraged them to embrace the boycott of West Indies sugar as it was women who

In the domestic department, they are the chief controllers, they, for the most part, provide the articles of family consumption; instead of purchasing that luxury, the cultivation of which constitutes at once the chief profits and oppressions of slavery, they can substitute that which is the genuine produce of free labour, and by so doing become a blessing to existing and unborn millions. (p. 6)

Women, in other words, were qualified 'not only to sympathise with suffering, but also to plead for the oppressed' (p. 4). Contrary to the assumption that boycotts by women were less important to the abolitionist movement, various historians such as Midgley (2007) have argued that the opposite was true. In many ways, women's abstention from slave-based products proved to be far more pivotal, as their actions demanded immediate emancipation as opposed to gradual change through political lobbying and petitioning.

Other notable examples of early consumer activism include various forms of food riots across the globe – typically driven by the threat of scarcity and inflation – which have typically relied on the mobilisations of women to demand more affordable and accessible subsistence. Although the gender balance of food riots has varied from time and place, women, by virtue of their place and role within household economies, have typically led such struggles and been pivotal in initiating new modes and tactics of collective action (e.g. Hunt, 2010). In 1911 Northern France, for instance, and faced with dramatic rises in the price of bread, eggs and butter, women marched to the markets in protest, demanding lower prices and throwing eggs and other items if their demands were not met. In larger towns, such spontaneous protests gave way to full-fledged riots with thousands of women battling with police and soldiers (Taylor, 1996).

Beyond such early forms of explicit consumer activism and resistance, marketing history is also replete with stories of activist women, as well as ordinary housewives, trying to live and consume differently. Many suffragettes were enthusiastic supporters of vegetarianism and frugal lifestyles that could, in today's terms, be described as early examples of 'voluntary simplicity' (Shaw and Newholm, 2002). As the historian Leah Leneman (1997) documents, many feminist publications of the early 20th century included images of women trying vegetarian recipes; in several suffragette branches there were lectures on topics such as 'the ethics of food reform', and demonstrations of 'vegetarian cookery' (p. 272). Beyond vegetarianism, feminist publications covered a range of other topics, from the ethics of frugal and egalitarian lifestyles to the animal cruelty involved in the decoration of Edwardian ladies' hats.

Finally, it is worth noting that women have been pioneers in what we now recognise as the broader 'ethical consumer' movement, the conscious and deliberate attempt to make certain positive consumption choices based on pro-social and pro-environmental beliefs and values (e.g. Crane et al., 2019). Within the UK, the first 'consumers league' was set up by the famous feminist and trade unionist Clementina Black to address concerns about retailers' labour conditions (Hilton, 2003). Members of the league were given a list of 'fair' dressmakers, milliners, shirtmakers and upholsterers operating within the vicinity of Bond Street, Oxford Street and Baker Street, and were asked to boycott those that were known for labour exploitation and unsafe working conditions. The league eventually failed, not least because, as Clementina Black explained, it was impossible to have a fully accurate and up-to-date guide at a large enough scale. Contemporary variants of such leagues, however, are numerous and can rely on a far wealthier pool of data and are far more sophisticated: these include, for instance, the 32-year-old UK magazine *Ethical Consumer* (https://www.ethicalconsumer.org/) and smartphone applications such as buycott.com.

On 7 September 2019, a blue plaque was unveiled at 45 Ship Street, Brighton in honour of a local woman who fought for improving the lives of working women (and arguably for bettering our consumption logics and practices), Clementina Black (see Figure 2.3). The plaque, according to local councillor Nancy Platts, also 'stands as a symbol to the hundreds of women who were part of this movement and whose names we will never know because they have been lost to history'.[4]

FEMALE ENTREPRENEURS AND THEIR MARKETING CREATIVITY

As previously mentioned, the entrepreneurial figure is often assumed to be male, the default standard against which women are measured and found wanting. Entrepreneurial creativity is thus associated with the idea of the male 'genius' – the light bulb moment – whereas female innovators are more likely to be identified with nurturing behaviours, 'seeding' an idea to take root (Elmore and Luna-Lucero, 2017). For this same reason, marketing textbooks feature fascinating tales of male entrepreneurs who

Figure 2.3   *The blue plaque commemorating Clementina Black*

took visionary approaches to markets more often than case studies of their female counterparts. Yet, as feminist business historians do their work, many amazing tales of entrepreneurial women emerge from the past; tales of women who were adept at spotting market opportunities and devising creative ways to maximise their potential.

Consider Eliza Luca Pinckney (1722–1793) who took over the management of her family's plantation in South Carolina, then a British colony, when she was only 16 and who is credited with changing agriculture in South Carolina. Showing incredible foresight for her young years, she recognised the potential of the indigo plant to provide dye for the fast-growing textile industry of the time. Her skills in cultivating, processing and marketing the indigo crop, as well as her generosity in sharing this knowledge with fellow agriculturalists, meant that indigo quickly became one of South Carolina's key export crops, second only to rice, its historical staple export.

Another entrepreneur with a distinct marketing flair was Lillian Vernon (1927–2015) who developed a niche market for personalised gifts and innovative gadgets that became a vast mail order empire. Fleeing Germany in 1937 because of the Nazis, she arrived in New York where she quickly established a business from small beginnings. Investing US$2,000 in leather handbags and belts with matching monographed heraldic crests, she targeted readers of a popular teenage magazine with great success. The resulting sales returned her investment eightfold, giving her the means to expand her product lines and reach a much wider market. By 1956 a mail order catalogue showcased her wares. Unlike big department store catalogues that sold a general range of goods, The Lillian Vernon Catalogue was first to specialise: the personalised products offered on its pages were unique as well as low-cost (Povich, 2015). To this end, Vernon regularly attended trade fairs and prided herself on her ability to discover ingenious items that would please her customers. Referred to as the 'Queen of Mail-order Catalogues' (Arnold, 2015), she was the first female founder to be traded on the American Stock Exchange when her company went public in 1987.

And let us not forget the marketing genius of French designer, Coco Chanel (1883–1971), whose iconic Little Black Dress became a fashion staple in every stylish woman's wardrobe. At the time of its introduction (1926) Chanel was defying lingering associations between black and mourning, a leftover from Victorian death rituals. Just as Henry Ford's Model T changed the car industry forever, so too did Chanel's Little Black Dress revolutionise fashion design, reflecting one of her abiding mottos 'Simplicity is the keynote of all elegance.'

The list of daring female entrepreneurs could easily continue but in what follows we explore the marketing expertise of two women in more depth, Madam C. J. Walker and Helena Rubinstein. Both these outstanding business leaders were also very gifted marketers. Yet, although they have both been featured in the work of sociologists and cultural historians, neither have to date been mentioned in marketing histories or textbook case studies, nor has their marketing ingenuity been sufficiently acknowledged. We intend to rectify this oversight in the two vignettes that follow.

MADAM C. J. WALKER: WONDERFUL HAIR GROWER FOR BLACK WOMEN

As the recent subject of a Netflix series, Madam C. J. Walker (1867–1919) has become a legend in contemporary popular culture as well as in the history of black activism. She is widely esteemed for her entrepreneurial brilliance together with her enduring legacy of philanthropic works. The first female self-made millionaire in the US, she certainly merits the documentation of her extraordinary life. From humble beginnings – she was born Sarah Breedlove on a Louisiana plantation – she overcame many trials and tribulations to found her own business based on a line of cosmetics and hair care products for black women. In so doing, she provided an important role model for the African American community in New York society at that time. Although much of her story has now been told, the marketing elements have not so far been investigated in any detail and these provide our focus here.

Finding herself a widow with a young daughter at only 20 years of age, Walker moved to St. Louis where she worked as a laundress for many years to support them both. During these years she suffered hair loss, a common problem among other black women due to harsh working conditions and poor nutrition. Walker experimented with various home remedies but then came across Annie Turnbo Malone's hair care products and found these helped cure her alopecia. She was so enthusiastic about the products that she became a sales agent for the company in 1904. The knowledge she gained during this time fuelled her desire to create her own hair-growing tonic. In 1906 she married again to C. J. Walker, branding her newly developed hair care line as Madam C. J. Walker's Wonderful Hair Grower. Referring to herself as 'Madam' connoted respectability and polite society, but more importantly it also evoked the French beauty industry and its associated prestige. To further cement this connection, she sometimes used the French spelling 'Madame'. Her marketing acumen was already evident in this implicit recognition of the value of brand image. But over and above her ability to carve an exceptional brand persona for her product line, it was surely her achievements as an early pioneer of network marketing methods that make her stand out from the marketing crowd of the time.

Initially she sold her products door to door, diligently reinvesting all her profits in new materials and newspaper advertising. Although in the early days she drew on her husband's expertise of marketing and advertising (gained as a sales agent in a newspaper), she quickly developed her own marketing skills, proclaiming his vision for the business to be too narrow (Koman, 2006). In fact, she was later to divorce Walker but always kept his name, no doubt mindful of the necessity for continuity of her brand image.

Her route to business expansion was the appointment of sales agents and she tirelessly travelled the country to establish a direct sales distribution network that grew to encompass more than 5,000 women selling her products throughout America. She recruited women from a broad range of backgrounds and the loyal team she built included hairdressers, schoolteachers, housewives, cooks and washerwomen (Koman, 2006). The genius of this sales network was not just its selling power, it also provided a way to overcome the racial restrictions of the day that prevented her distributing through drugstores, the normal outlet for such products. As such, Walker functioned as an activist entrepreneur (Hasan et al., 2020), fighting for the rights of African American people, an activism that she pursued all her life even when she became one of the wealthy elite. She was known as a 'prominent and vocal activist' (Hasan et al., 2020, p. 342) and used every opportunity she could to promote a more equitable society for people of colour.

Putting her principles into practice, her sales agents were well-rewarded and she never ceased to encourage her black female sales force to better themselves and to strive for independence. With the setting up of training centres dedicated to the Walker System of Hair Care, she nurtured a national sales force, making her agents aware of the need to empathise with clients and pamper them. They received intensive training in hair care and beauty techniques, including how to apply scalp treatments and hair restylings as well as other body maintenance therapies such as manicures and massages. In addition, they learned business skills such as account management as well as how best to use the space within their home to create a small salon where they could receive clients. By 1917 Walker was holding yearly conventions for her sales agents where she could not only make them familiar with new sales and beauty techniques, but also energise and motivate them. The passion she had for her enterprise and its products, together with her activist identity, made her a truly inspirational figure, prompting her vast team of loyal agents to see her as a black role model they could look up to and even emulate.

Brand culture involves all the aspects and connotations of a brand that makes it an important part of everyday life and experience. Through the enthusiasm and dedication of her sales agents, Walker built an incredibly strong and unique brand culture around her enterprise, a culture that was based on shared progressive ideals that helped her fellow African Americans to transcend the systematic racism they encountered in their everyday lives.

In 2013, a Unilever subsidiary, Sundial Brands bought the rights to the Madam C. J. Walker brand (with her great-granddaughter's approval). Comprising a product line of shampoos, conditioners and hair masks,

Sundial relaunched the brand as Madam C. J. Walker Beauty Culture (BBC News, 2020). Most recently, in 2018, Sundial's co-founder, Richelieu Dennis, purchased Walker's historic mansion (with 34 rooms) and its huge estate in Irvington, New York, with the aim of using the venue as a space for black female entrepreneurs to develop their ideas and find support. Madam C. J. Walker's legacy lives on!

HELENA RUBINSTEIN: MARKETING BEAUTY AS POWER

Standard marketing textbooks (Kotler, for example) often quote Charles Revson (1906–1975) – known as a pioneer in the cosmetics industry and creator of the Revlon brand – highlighting the marketing acumen revealed by his famous phrase 'In the factory we make cosmetics, in the drugstore we sell hope.' His shrewd advice, hinting at the transformative potential of marketing messages, initiates many a marketing student into the symbolic aspects of consumer behaviour. Yet, in the same textbooks, we hear little of his arch-rival, Helena Rubinstein, a Polish immigrant to the US, who built a cosmetics empire before Revson. Her business prowess and widely acknowledged marketing expertise made her one of the first self-made female entrepreneurs in the US to be worth US$1million. Rather than selling hope to women, Revson's somewhat patronising approach to his female consumers, Rubinstein's celebrated strapline, 'Beauty is Power' offered women inner confidence and empowerment through wearing make-up. Whereas Revson's missive evokes feminine foibles, Rubinstein's conveys feminine strength and potential.

As such, Rubinstein is credited with changing how women viewed themselves and with playing a major role in influencing modern tastes and styles (Klein, 2014). She democratised the beauty industry, making the use of cosmetics widely accepted and accessible. Prior to Rubinstein, beauty had been the preserve of a wealthy elite who frowned on the use of cosmetics, associating it with the behaviours of actresses and call girls. For most of the 1800s only hydrating creams for a smoother skin were considered acceptable, as well as the occasional skin whitener. With the increasing popularity of photography and film from the early 1900s onwards, however, all this began to change. Thanks to American women wanting a little bit of Hollywood glamour for themselves, the use of make-up became increasingly popular, particularly among those women newly entering the workforce. Notably, suffragettes used red lipstick as a gesture of defiance in their 1912 march for the vote along New York's

Fifth Avenue. By the end of World War 1, spurred on by the invention of the push-up lipstick metal tube, previously denigrated red lipstick was becoming mainstream. The 'New Woman' of the 1920s was about to arrive, a woman who valued her own independence and believed in her right to self-determination. It was this market that brought Helena Rubinstein enduring success.

Born in Kraków, Poland, the eldest of eight daughters, she had moved to Australia in her early 20s to live with her uncle after a dispute with her father about who she should marry. Once there she started selling Crème Valaze, a beauty cream made following her mother's special formula combining herbs, almonds and fir tree extract. It proved so popular with local women that before long she was able to open her own shop in Melbourne. In 1908 she opened a salon in London and, shortly after that, another in Paris. By 1916, Rubinstein had also opened a salon in New York. Further expansion followed rapidly with salons in many other US cities as well as sales of her products in major department stores. All this while she was also a mother, giving birth to two sons in 1909 and 1912 respectively, having married a Polish American journalist in 1908. Nothing could slow Rubinstein's market development down. By 1917, she had taken on both the manufacturing and wholesale distribution of her products as well.

But her marketing genius is what interests us in this short case study. Her blend of self-branding, with luxury positioning for her products, was quite exceptional for the time and she introduced many innovative features that remain pertinent in contemporary consumer culture. These include spectacular settings for her salons with luxurious packaging for her products and the glamour of celebrity endorsements, an extravagant mix that has led to her salon openings being described as 'theatrical galas' (Clifford, 2003, p. 101).

Rubinstein's self-branding was key to the success of her cosmetics empire. She managed her public image astutely, taking every opportunity to demonstrate those values she wished to have associated with the Rubinstein product brand. In doing so, it is evident she perceived the two – her image and that of her product range – as intricately intertwined. Accordingly, she emphasised those aspects of her lifestyle, personality and interests that she believed would give her business a strong differentiation in the marketplace.

As part of her self-branding strategy, she built what we would now term an 'origin myth' (Arnould and Thompson, 2015) around herself: the Polish immigrant whose initial success rested on her mother's unique formula that incorporated rare herbs from the Carpathian mountains of Rubinstein's homeland. Rubinstein was thus no stranger to the role of brand authenticity, and she seems to have understood intuitively the affective power of storytelling to better connect with customers and build brand loyalty. A crucial component of her origin myth was the thwarted intention of her youth to go to medical school. Instead, she devoted herself to the 'science' of cosmetics. In publicity shots, she frequently emphasised the quasi-scientific nature of her endeavours by appearing in a white coat, attire usually portrayed by men in advertisements to convey a rational, authoritative voice that builds trust. Similarly, Rubinstein used the lab-coat look to symbolise her authority about cosmetics and skin tones. Indeed, one of her genius innovations in the industry was the introduction of different cosmetics for differing skin tones.

Nonetheless, her most influential marketing innovation was surely the creation of a compelling sense of place for the brand through her beauty salons and their lavish decor. In contrast to the more clinical-looking layouts used by competitors, Rubinstein's spectacular salons resembled opulent boudoirs combining eclectic mixes of fashion and art within their extravagant surrounds (Clifford, 2003). Known to be an avid collector of art, Rubinstein displayed many of her acquisitions in the salons. In this way, her acknowledged expertise in the art world was interwoven into her entrepreneurial identity, reinforcing her impeccable taste and sense of style. Rubinstein maximised publicity opportunities whenever she could, and her exclusive salons featured regularly in *Vogue* on account of the visual delights they presented to readers. Significantly, turning her salons into display venues meant clients experienced not only the beauty services offered but also an inculcation of European tastes and modernist art. As such, Rubinstein played a major role in determining the fashionable femininity of the era (Clifford, 2003) as well as being at the avant-garde of experiential marketing.

The connections she established with celebrities further reinforced her competence in the public's eye to dictate feminine tastes and style. She tapped into the growing American fascination with silent movies and a concomitant obsession with actresses such as Gloria Swanson, Mary Pickford and Joan Crawford. Stars of the early cinema like these popularised the use of make-up among the middle classes and their beauty routines were frequently discussed in fashion magazines of the time. Rubinstein got many famous screen actresses to endorse her brand. She even designed a special kohl eyeliner for the American sex symbol Theda Bara who wished to dramatise her eyes to show off her face to full advantage. Hence, Rubinstein's creation of the 'Vamp' look, so called on account of Bara's role as a vampire in one of her films.

Apart from her trademark eye pencil and mascara, Rubinstein led other innovations in the beauty industry. She introduced the 'Day of Beauty', an idea that encouraged women to spend longer immersed in what Rubinstein promoted as 'a world of beauty'. Combining overall health assessments with exercise routines, leisure facilities and beauty treatments, the concept was an instant success and spread rapidly to her other salons around the world. In 1936, when she opened her new Fifth Avenue salon in New York, it included a gym, cinema, restaurant, library, solarium and a hairdressing salon, as well as all the beauty treatment rooms.

So to summarise, Helen Rubinstein demonstrated a marketing expertise way ahead of her time; an expertise that enabled her to readily identify new market opportunities and take creative approaches to their development. Early on she recognised the power of self-branding in conjunction with celebrity endorsement, as well as the importance of tapping into the cultural zeitgeist. In Rubinstein's case, this zeitgeist was the increasing momentum of women's rights and the quest for more female autonomy. Like the department stores before her, she created spaces for women that legitimised them going out in public without male escorts, spaces that, in turn, also encouraged female freedom and independence. Rubinstein maximised every available marketing opportunity that came her way. When she married for the second time to Artchil Gourielli-Tchkonia, a Georgian prince 23 years her junior, she subsequently named a male cosmetics line after him, The House of Gourielli. She was most certainly one of the foremost influences on the development of the cosmetics industry and there can be no doubt that she deserves to be recognised as an early marketing guru, an accolade rarely given to a woman. Let us not forget her, or indeed her fellow entrepreneur, Madame C. J. Walker, in our marketing textbooks!

NOTES

1. The material in this section and the two that follow was first presented in a keynote address entitled Polyphonic Marketing: Breaking the Silences presented at the 52nd Academy of Marketing Conference July 2019.
2. https://www.bitchmedia.org/article/what-happened-to-home-economics -history-feminism-education (last accessed 1 November 2021).
3. http://abolition.e2bn.org/campaign_17.html (last accessed 1 November 2021).

4. https://www.brightonandhovenews.org/2019/09/13/a-blue-plaque-for
   -suffragist-clementina-black/ (last accessed 1 November 2021).

3. Marketing communications: selling or smashing stereotypes?

Marketing communications in general – but especially advertising campaigns and printed materials – are saturated with a myriad of stereotypes typically involving categories of gender, race and socio-economic grouping. To be sure, many images are so transparent we can simply mock them, but many are not. They often influence us in nuanced ways that go under the radar, shaping our views and ideas of what is 'normal'. The surfeit of stereotypical imagery generated by marketing messages led to the Advertising Standards Authority (ASA) ruling in 2019 that 'marketing communications must not include gender stereotypes that are likely to cause harm, or serious widespread offence'. The ASA based its decision on much evidence showing how advertisements reinforce outdated views about men and women's roles, capabilities and behaviours; views that impede gender equality and cause financial, physical and emotional harm. Philadelphia cheese and Volkswagen were the first brands to fall foul of the new ruling. The former's ad took a comic approach, depicting two new fathers left holding their babies in a restaurant. Tempted by the appetising morsels revolving on the food conveyor belt, they set their infants on it while they indulge themselves. In a comic moment, after they have paused to relish the great taste of the Philadelphia cheese, they rush to seize their babies who continue to circle on the conveyor amid the food. The ASA upheld complaints that accused the ad of perpetuating harmful stereotypes by suggesting men were irresponsible childcarers. Volkswagen's ad for an electric eGolf depicted various scenes: two male astronauts, a male para-athelete, a male and a female climber in a tent suspended on a rock face and a woman sitting on a park bench by a pram. Once again the ASA banned the ad for portraying women in passive positions (the female climber was asleep) while the men, in contrast, were shown to be adventurous and facing challenges.

This chapter explores such stereotyping in more depth through the lens of key sociological and cultural theorists, namely Erving Goffman, Laura Mulvey and Judith Butler. As we scrutinise what their theories tell us about the gendered nature of many marketing messages and campaigns, we also ponder how effectively marketers can challenge traditional stereotypes and their concomitant social portrayals. One such ubiquitous theme is female empowerment. Our purpose here is to reveal how this postfeminist discourse simultaneously 'incorporates and repudiates feminist ideals, neutralizing feminism's political force' (Catterall, Maclaran and Stevens, 2005; Windels et al., 2020, p. 18). To this end we use Rottenberg's (2018) concept of neoliberal feminism to delve deeper into femvertising and expose the ideological underpinnings of empowerment advertising messages. Tropes of freedom, equality and justice abound in current marketing strategies, and we critique these not only for femmewashing, but also greenwashing, pinkwashing, whitewashing and even carewashing. At issue here is how such messages often serve to only profit the patriarchy. Accordingly, we put this laundry list of washings under the spotlight and reveal the ways in which the list expands exponentially as corporations struggle to convey global images of diversity and inclusion.

GENDER AS PERFORMANCE

Insofar as the famous sociologist and social psychologist Erving Goffman did not consider himself a feminist theorist, it may seem a little strange to commence this section with an overview of his work. Nonetheless, it is fair to say that his theories around social interactions have certainly had a profound and lasting impact on feminist thinking (West, 1996) and, hence, our reason for including him here. A leading proponent of symbolic interactionism, Goffman is best known for the concept of dramaturgy, the theatrical representation of life that he expounded in his 1956 book, *The Presentation of Self in Everyday Life*. In this work he divided human behaviours into front stage, back stage and offstage, arguing that social interaction is greatly influenced by its audience as well as by the time and place where it is conducted.

His theory of impression management proposed that individuals base a front stage identity performance on the self they believe is appropriate for their audience. In other words, a sense of self is the outcome of how we manage our self-impressions in any specific social context. According to Goffman, our performances are primed to seek favourable feedback from those around us. Despite his emphasis on psychology, he did not ignore the importance of common cultural practices, being convinced that the values, norms and beliefs of any given social group also determined such identity performances. Thus, front of stage performances are framed within the 'principles of organization that govern events' (Goffman, 1986, p. 10); frames determined by the dominant social order that guide how individuals interpret actions. Such framing determines the limitations and expectations placed on what type of performance we can give and gender frames, being a key element in social ordering, are no different. From Goffman's perspective, 'gender identity is an illusory artefact of the available schedule for the portrayal of gender' (Brickell, 2003, p. 160).

For Goffman, therefore, gender is part of the performance of impression management. Just as he does not acknowledge any core self, independent of social interaction, so too he does not conceive of maleness or femaleness as a natural biological given. Indeed, Goffman also eschews the sex/gender distinction that had been very important to feminist thought since Oakley (1972), a distinction that has also been dismantled in later feminist theorising (Butler, 1993). Like Butler, Goffman argues that both sex and gender are socially constructed, and that differentiation based on sex (male/female) is as much a categorising social practice as the attributes associated with those categories (masculine/feminine).

Overall, however, Goffman's work focuses on a micro analysis of the gestural and linguistic aspects of human interactions as they are played out in everyday life through systems of practice, conventions and procedural rules that guide and organise any given communication moment (Goffman, 1956). His quest is to establish what understandings exist about who is allowed to initiate a particular type of conversation, together with what topics are permissible. Other specifics such as when and where such interactions can take place, how long someone is allowed to speak, who interrupts and what gestures are conveyed, are all significant features of his analysis. All these micro aspects of daily interactions have been very important to the feminist agenda of 'the personal is political', revealing as they do the processes whereby gender bias is unconsciously encoded and perpetuated through social interactions. But it was Goffman's later study, *Gender Advertisements* (1979) that was to supply the empirical support for the many feminist critiques that had already challenged the representation of women in advertising. His book identified gender stereotyping in North American advertisements across a range of products, highlighting the gendered nature of the stylised poses that denoted masculinity or femininity. Goffman's work exposed how men were most likely to be depicted as confident and in charge, whereas women were shown as vulnerable and submissive. Stylistic techniques could achieve this impression: showing men filling the space in contrast to the more contracted demeanors of their female counterparts.

Goffman's study thus gave influential sociological support to feminist claims of advertising's gender biases. Yet, despite the advertising industry's drive from the 1980s onwards to feature more diverse masculinities and femininities that avoid stereotyping, it is disappointing to note that the rate of any real change is slow. There have been various studies over the years highlighting how little has really altered in terms of male and female representations. One Australian study (Bell and Milic, 2002) undertook a semiotic analysis of 827 magazine advertisements using Goffman's principles and concluded that gender bias still occurred across perspectival angle, plane of composition and gaze. Another study concluded that gender stereotyping continued to be commonplace in German television advertising (Knoll, Eisend and Steinhagen, 2011). The most frequent portrayals of women were younger, inside the domestic environment and in a dependent role. Conversely, male representations were likely to be older, outside of the home and in independent roles. And yet again, in their analysis of the *Good Housekeeping* magazine between 1950 and 2010, Marshall et al. (2014) found that, despite broadening depictions of the breadwinner roles in advertisements, in the main they reinforced traditional paternal masculinities.

While most of the research on gender stereotyping in advertising emphasises the biases in depicting women, there is a pressing need for more masculinity studies to understand the limitations gender stereotyping also places on men. Advertising can, of course, likewise affect men's self-esteem and engender feelings of inadequacy (Zayer and Otnes, 2012). Significantly, Gentry and Harrison (2010) discovered that advertising tends to put men in more egalitarian roles when targeting a female audience. Consequently, such representations are not seen by men and therefore have little impact on male attitudes and behaviours more widely. Hence, these authors call for more active male portrayals of fatherhood in ads that target a male audience. Of course, a recent Gillette campaign (2019), 'We Believe: The Best Men Can Be', tried to do exactly this with mixed consequences! Within a week of the ad's release on the brand's YouTube channel, it had garnered 749,000 dislikes compared with 386,000 likes (Cross, 2019). And Brandwatch pointed out that although Gillette received more than 1.4 million mentions in the first week on social media and it commenced more positively, by the end of the week negative comments dominated. Unlike other brands known for their social activism, Gillette has long had a 'rugged masculinity' approach to its market and many people accused the brand of hypocrisy and inauthenticity. We will discuss more about what is termed 'femme-washing' and 'queerwashing' later in this chapter.

All these studies point to the continued relevance of Goffman's theories on advertising's role in gender stereotyping and the importance of subjecting advertising and marketing communications – in terms of content, format, style and linguistic devices – to these types of micro analyses. In addition, there is a need for staff in advertising agencies to recognise the damage that stereotypes can cause and the role agencies can play in bringing about change. An insightful study conducted with advertising professionals identified historical discourses of gender and vulnerability influencing the creative and strategic decision-making processes (Zayer and Coleman, 2015). Such discourses not only reinforced stereotypical notions of women being particularly susceptible to persuasive marketing messaging, but also implied that men were somehow immune to this type of seduction.

THE MALE GAZE

In the previous section we saw how Goffman conceived of gender differences as being produced by social practices, rather than being 'natural'. Nonetheless, despite his acknowledgement that these differences are unequal and usually work to men's advantage (Brickell, 2003), he did not interrogate gender power relations in greater depth. For this reason Laura Mulvey's work is important because she exposed the scopic regimes that underpin these power relations. As such, her work is especially significant in the visual domain of advertising. Mulvey draws on feminist theory, psychoanalysis and film studies to theorise what she terms 'the male gaze' or, more specifically, the heterosexual masculine gaze. In her seminal paper, 'Visual Pleasure and Narrative Cinema' (Mulvey, 1975), she made a cutting critique of Hollywood cinema's patriarchal ideology in representing women as 'other', always an object and never a subject. The camera gaze, she argued, reflected a male gaze that was most likely to focus on male actions (the male hero) and female appearances, particularly to emphasise the erotic impact of the latter. The male gaze thus constructs a power imbalance that perpetuates women's sexual objectification and the patriarchal status quo.

Like Goffman, Mulvey's theorising exposes the active/passive binary underpinning the gaze, while also exploring more deeply the voyeuristic pleasure of objectifying women. Her emphasis is on the sexual pleasure

– the 'scopophilia', according to Freudian theory – that the male viewer experiences through looking at the female. In this respect she shares much with Berger whose influential book *Ways of Seeing* (1972) proposed women's experience of the gaze to be dramatically different from that of men. He highlighted how women are condemned to continually watch themselves (the male in her) and the surveyed (herself). She is thus cast in a self-obsessed and passive role that sharply contrasts with the more self-possessed and active role of her male counterpart.

Mulvey sees these processes as placing a huge burden on women, especially because of the ways that the male gaze reinforces Freud's Madonna/whore binary as a mode of cultural stereotyping that positions women as either promiscuous temptresses or chaste virgins. These polarised perceptions of women remain relevant today. A study of 108 heterosexual Israeli men (Bareket et al., 2018) revealed how men who endorsed this dichotomy were more likely to support patriarchal social structures. Unsurprisingly, these men also reported lower romantic relationship satisfaction!

Scopophilia also underpins the notion of the 'carnal feminine' (Stevens and Maclaran, 2008). Advertising narratives frequently depict women in a carnal light, behaving in a sensual or sexual way that represents women as being controlled by their bodily desires. Think of the iconic British chocolate brand, Cadbury Flake, whose advertising has a long history of showing women in suggestive positions savouring the chocolate bar. One famous Cadbury Flake commercial (1988) portrayed a woman on her windowsill, dressed only in her lingerie, slowly eating the chocolate, while in another (1992), the bath overflows as she revels in her treat. The connotations with oral sex have not gone unnoticed and, on occasions, Cadbury's Flake advertisements have been banned for this reason. Behind this recurrent trope in advertising is the idea that women get more erotic pleasure from food than men and that they give in readily to their sinful cravings, a hypersexualisation that evokes the promiscuous side of the Freudian dichotomy.

Despite this continuing relevance, much later work has developed Mulvey's initial theorising and shown how the male gaze is only one of multiple subject positions that spectators may adopt. To be fair, Mulvey was exploring mainstream classic Hollywood cinema, and this does not necessarily transpose well to other cultural contexts. For example, in relation to hegemonic masculinity,[1] Mulvey's contention that male spectators make a narcissistic identification with images of other men is an oversimplification when we consider lifestyle advertising images that cause men to engage with their own bodies. Patterson and Elliott (2002) illustrate how this inversion of the gaze, reflecting a more feminised masculinity (think David Beckham here!), may result in differing subject positions that lead to rejection, identification or even desire. Furthermore, the readers in their study sometimes iterated between these positions, as might be expected when we bear in mind that identity is an ongoing and unfinished process.

As regards female spectators, too, various feminist critics of Mulvey's work have argued for a more active conceptualisation that resists the male gaze and recognises the agency of the 'female gaze' (Gammam and Marshment, 1988). Consider the quintessentially feminist blockbuster, *Thelma and Louise* (1991), which challenges Hollywood's patriarchal gaze with its mocking tones and feisty heroines. Cooper (2000, p. 277) identifies two key narrative devices that structure the film's strong female gaze: 'depicting men as spectacles for women's attention; and the celebration of women's friendships'. Cooper concludes that these devices of mockery challenge, resist and defy patriarchy, thereby inviting a feminist reading. Similarly, contemporary advertising is now replete with advertising representations of women that convey female agency, especially sexual agency (Gill, 2008), and use comparable narrative devices. Here we can think back to the famous Coca-Cola Diet Coke commercials that played a leading role in this respect. In the first and most iconic one – 'Diet Coke Break' (1994) – a female gaze pokes fun at the traditional male perspective as a group of female office workers feast their eyes on a gorgeous construction worker below their window. They watch lasciviously as he slowly removes his shirt in the heat of the day to drink his Diet Coke and the powerful voice of rhythm and blues singer, Etta James, belts out the advertisement's soundtrack, 'I just wanna make love to you'. This reversal of stereotypically passive female portrayals was a huge success, resonating with the rise of neoliberal feminism during the 1990s (see later discussions in this chapter) and setting the scene for many other copycat advertisements. Coca-Cola's campaign continued with the 'window washer' in 1997, the 'elevator engineer' in 2007 and the 'gardener' in 2013.

Intersectional implications of the gaze hitherto ignored, such as race and sexuality, are increasingly recognised as salient factors. Take, for example, the white aesthetic dominating film and television in Western culture, an aesthetic that ensures whiteness is the norm and blackness is experienced as other (hooks, 1992). Over the past ten years, there has been a move to include more diverse casting as evidenced in the Netflix

2020 hit series, *Bridgerton*, a Regency drama that contained a variety of black actors (including the leading male) and actresses, presenting a challenge to the taken-for-granted whiteness of aristocratic portrayals in historical dramas. Similarly, although much advertising has reinforced the 'white gaze' (Wallowitz, 2008; Davis, 2021), there have been significant improvements in recent times. Nevertheless, Davis's (2018) detailed review of marketing theories and practices reveals a long-standing racism in marketing and highlights how some common marketing messages still reinforce the superiority of whiteness. For instance, in 2017 the Nivea brand received much criticism for promoting a deodorant with the tagline 'white is purity'. And Unilever has only recently, in 2020, renamed its 'Fair and Lovely' range, even while it continues to sell its skin-whitening cream frequently castigated for perpetuating negative stereotypes about darker skin colours.

The 'queer gaze' has relevance too for understanding how LGBTQI+ audiences interpret visual materials (Evans and Gamman, 1995). To this end, Kates (2000) identifies three types of scopophilic pleasures through which gay men may experience the consumption of mainstream cinema: 'resistant' pleasures through deriving alternative meanings; complicit or 'guilty' pleasures that partake in a dominant set of socio-cultural meanings; and identificatory pleasures that evoke empathy with characters and their dilemmas. More recently Nolke (2018) undertook an intersectional analysis of explicit LGBTQI+ portrayals in mainstream advertising between 2009 and 2015. She found that despite a large increase in explicit representations of LGBTQI+ characters, 230 out of 240 intersections of sexuality, class, age and race remain invisible. Notably, she draws attention to the perpetuation of a 'heteronormative, domesticized version of "gayness"'. This point brings us neatly to the next section and Judith Butler's exposure of heteronormativity as a pivotal power mechanism that locates subjectivities within their broader societal context.

GENDER PERFORMATIVITY

Turning to Butler once again (see Chapter 1), in this section we first distinguish her concept of performativity from that of Goffman's performance, before returning to her heteronormative matrix and its implications for marketing communications. Certainly, there is often confusion between performativity and performance especially on account of the contention by Goffman, as well as Butler, that biological sex is also a social construction subsumed by gender (Brickell, 2003). This has been sometimes taken to mean that there is no sex, only gender and that gender is therefore a choice, something to be decided on a daily basis (Butler, Osbourne and Segal, 1994). But neither theorist wishes to imply this, simply agreeing that both sex and gender are socially constructed, and sex is not somehow more 'natural'. Crucially, Butler is at pains to emphasise that performativity is not a choice but rather: 'has to do with repetition, very often the repetition of oppressive and painful gender norms . . . This is not freedom but a question of how to work the trap that one is inevitably in' (interview with Liz Kotz, 1992).

The key difference between Butler and Goffman is at an ontological level, however, and they disagree over the agency of the self. Whereas Goffman sees the self as emerging from the performance of social inter-actions, Butler rejects the idea of a self entirely (Brickell, 2003). Strongly influenced by Foucault (1977), she denies the notion of a pre-existing subject, arguing that performance, in its ongoing reiteration of norms, constitutes the subject; a subject that is continually produced and repro-duced in discourse. Performativity is the process whereby a speech act, or utterance in Butler's terminology, creates events or relations in the world (such as pronouncing the sex of a child at birth).

Moving beyond Foucault, Butler emphasises the significance of embodied doings, as practices that are embedded in specific historical and cultural discourses. In this way identity is 'performatively constituted by the very "expressions" that are said to be its results' (Butler, 1990, p. 25). Consequently, for Butler, the 'forced repetition' of previous doings is how they become naturalised as socio-cultural codes and norms. Such naturalisation then determines who is judged a subject worthy of recogni-tion and who is excluded (Fraser and Honneth, 2003). This is very much Nolke's (2018) point about the heteronormative portrayals of gay people in advertising discussed in the previous section. For this reason too, lesbian feminist Monique Wittig (1980) argues 'lesbians are not women'. In so doing she challenges the taken-for-granted nature of a heterosexual system where the biological differentiation of men and women functions to validate what Wittig terms 'the heterosexual contract' and women's inferior status. Thus interventions and resignifications that disrupt rep-etitions of the heteronormative matrix are possible and marketing com-munications have the potential to play a major role in this respect. Just as marketing messages are often seen to reinforce stereotypes, so too have they the power to change these stereotypes and to act as resignifications in the Butlerian sense as illustrated in the example that follows.

The Super Bowl is one of America's most watched TV transmissions and, hence, a much-prized advertising spot. In February 2018, the arena's digital screens featured Coca-Cola's high-profile commercial that provoked plenty of buzz on social media with its non-binary gender reference. Entitled, 'The Wonder of Us', many diverse and colourful characters drink Coca-Cola as the voiceover explains: 'there's a coke for he and she and her and me and them'. As the gender-neutral pronoun 'them' is mentioned, our focus is drawn to someone with a rainbow lanyard around their neck. In so doing, Coca-Cola communicated its support of the LGBTQI+ community to over 100 million people, as well as taking steps towards normalising gender non-conformity (Allen, 2018).

As we can see, Coca-Cola's high-profile Super Bowl advertisement marks a bold 'resignification' in terms of the heteronormative matrix that normalises opposite sex desire. In breaking with expected heteronormative norms by adding another sexual category, the advertisement interrupts the expected repetition, while putting across the advertisement's message of support for diversity in its many guises. Yet, the commercial carefully steers away from being too didactically 'woke', instead showing people going about their everyday lives as different voices contribute to the poetic narrative in reinforcement of Coca-Cola's unifying theme. This understated way of including 'them' in the campaign makes for acceptance rather than stigmatisation by its audience.

Of course, it remains to be seen how effective resignifying moments are, which depends on their repetition over time. Butler highlights the multitude of institutional and cultural practices that sustain the discourse of heteronormativity, practices that go unquestioned in our daily lives. Significantly, though, because gender is something we *do* rather than *have*, our ideas of masculinity and femininity – as well as the very binary on which they are based – can change because of actions that subvert rather than reinforce gender norms. As previously mentioned (Chapter 1), Thompson and Üstüner (2015) illustrate the 'ideological edgework' women's roller derby skaters undertake that challenges ideals of femininity. Coca-Cola too has a history of contributing to changing notions of femininity with its advertising in the early part of the 20th century placing continual emphasis on models of progressive American femininity, a model that was more individualistic and realised through consumption.

Yet, Coca-Cola's most famed resignifying moment must surely remain the inversion of the male gaze in its iconic Diet Coke commercials of the 1990s. Against a background of feminist activism targeting advertising's limited representations of women and their bodies, these campaigns were the vanguard of the many female empowerment themes that emerged in advertising during this period and that persist to present times. The end of the 20th century saw images of female empowerment proliferate in advertising more widely, with the repackaging of 'feminist quests for freedom, choice and opportunity as images, desires, lifestyles, and emotions that can be attained through consumption', as McDonald (2000, p. 38) so succinctly puts it. In the section that follows we go on to problematise images of female empowerment with a discussion of how neoliberal feminism (Rottenberg, 2018) exposes the limitations of any positive structural change arising from such images.

NEOLIBERAL FEMINISM

Fast forwarding a couple of decades, female empowerment has become a mainstream theme in marketing and PR campaigns: from Dove's famous Real Beauty and Evolution campaigns to Emma Watson's and Beyonce's enthusiastic embrace of the F-word. For various social critics (e.g. Rottenberg, 2014, 2018; Banet-Weiser, 2018) this is not a coincidence but the last act in the ongoing commodification, if not political 'righting' (Farris and Rottenberg, 2017), of feminist principles and ideas. The key issue with so-called neoliberal (Rottenberg, 2014) or popular (Banet-Weiser, 2018) feminism is that it superficially engages with ideas of female empowerment whilst shying away from the deep-rooted socio-economic and political causes of gendered and intersectional injustices.

In the archetypal neoliberal feminist logic, women need to overcome any feelings of vulnerability, victimhood and even interdependence and get on top of their game, not least by following the advice of an ever-expanding list of neoliberal feminist heroines: from former Princeton University professor Anne-Marie Slaughter's 'Why women still can't have it all' (2012) and Facebook's Chief Operating Officer Sheryl Sandberg's *Lean In: Women, Work and The Will to Lead* (2013) to Ivanka Trump's *Women Who Work: Rewriting the Rules for Success* (2017). Underlying such manifestos is a far more 'competitive' (McRobbie, 2015), entrepreneurial and decidedly individualist notion of female empowerment, one that relies on continuously investing in one's self-brand or specs of 'human capital' (Brown, 2015).

For neoliberal feminists, nothing escapes the logic of such calculative investment: from carefully choosing one's networks and friendships to engaging in social causes and 'social enterprises' in so far as they are good for one's CV. Put differently, in neoliberal feminism's most extreme articulation, the commodification of female empowerment has gone full circle, with women themselves behaving like commodities. The art of life is reduced to choosing among different interests, activities and relationships, above all on the basis of how enhancing they are to the best version of themselves, seen as an individual brand or enterprise. Through continuous labour and perseverance women can make it just like men do. Equally, they are solely responsible for failing to do so. No wonder then that many famous feminist scholars and activists (e.g. Fraser, 2013; Segal, 2017) have long pointed out that popular feminism is perfectly compatible with the powers that it purports to hold to account. It is primarily a version that has served a seemingly progressive, white, middle-class constituency that happens to be female, yet it is primarily interested in grabbing power, rather than distributing it more equally. For critics, neoliberal feminism has given feminism a bad name (Arruzza et al., 2019). It has colonised feminist themes whilst remaining unashamedly blinded to questions of economic and racial justice, among others (Hamad, 2020).

Despite being seen as a misappropriation of feminism, neoliberal feminism has found considerable popularity and enthusiasm in the marketplace. It has provided a viable route to profitability, one that relies on market-mediated empowerment through an ever-expanding list of gender, sex and body-positive slogans, from Dove's 'Real Beauty' to Always' 'Like a Girl' to Wranglers' 'More Than a Bum'. Also known as 'femvertising', this new genre of advertising consistently questions female gender stereotypes – even if somewhat ironically, they are the same stereotypes that, to a great extent, have been created by advertising. Generally, it has been very positively received by some target audiences (Akestam et al., 2017). Going back to Butler's ideas of performativity it is easy to see why this style of advertising has resonated with many women. Building on earlier examples of resignification, such as the Diet Coke advert, contemporary femvertising challenges what it means to be a woman and in doing so it offers a viable route to liberation from rigid heteronormativity.

Furthermore, in its more contemporary iterations, femvertising seems to be increasingly aware of the intersecting nature of systemic oppression (Sobande, 2019). It has become part of and, indeed, is often fully conflated with a broader queer and woke advertising movement that is alert to markers of privilege and discrimination, not only based on female sexuality but also other positionings along the axes of gender(s) and race. Building on the performativity of gender, queer advertising destabilises cis- and heteronormative representations and works beyond problematic dualisms (Kates, 1999) to expose less naturalised ways of (gendered) being. Archetypal examples include the aforementioned Gillette's 2019 'The Best Men Can Be' campaign, which takes a strong stance against toxic masculinity, all within the context of a brand that has historically relied on more patriarchal notions of manhood and masculinity. Much contemporary advertising also relies on implicit queering by, for instance, including gay iconography in otherwise mainstream adverts and hence aiming to appeal to both queer and mainstream audiences (Oakenfull and Greenlee, 2005). Queer advertising is often subsumed under so-called 'woke advertising' given that differences based on race also intersect with sexuality to further inhibit human flourishing (Rumens, 2017). A typical woke campaign would be Nike's Black Lives Matter series of adverts, including those featuring NFL quarterback Colin Kaepernick, or Pepsi's less successful attempt to engage with the same movement by featuring Kendal Jenner gifting a Pepsi to a policeman whilst at a protest. Despite their mixed results, woke and queer ads are believed to appeal to younger generations of consumers that are more politically aware, sceptical of the role of corporations, and largely averse to corporations that are believed to generate negative social and environmental impacts.[2]

The broader cultural context of such campaigns is the mainstreaming of intersectional awareness – evident, for instance, in recent Netflix series such as *Bridgerton* (mentioned above) but also *The Bold Type*, a comedy-drama series that follows three young friends as they rise up the corporate ladder in a contemporary women's magazine reminiscent of *Cosmopolitan*. Compared to the kind of *Sex and the City* version of neoliberal feminism, the protagonists of *The Bold Type* seem to be less individualist, in solidarity with each other, and invested in a variety of diversity issues. And yet, one could argue that this model of feminism remains neoliberal, albeit of a more enlightened, woke nature. The protagonists are interested in making it to the top because they all happen to be talented and surrounded by multiple opportunities for economic and cultural transition. However appealing, such narratives work to reproduce meritocratic ideals that are blind to the barriers many people face in entering the corporate world (let alone succeed in it) in the first place (Littler, 2017). Perhaps unwittingly, they thus reproduce 'colour-blind' and 'post-racial' ideologies which imply that people can choose to transcend systemic patriarchy and racism in the workplace and beyond (e.g.

Sobande, 2019). By implication, they are also individually responsible for failing to do so, as noted above.

There is also a broader economic context to contemporary forms of gendered, queer and woke advertising. Series such as *The Bold Type* and adverts such as Gillette's and Nike's have emerged in tandem with so-called 'compassionate' (Benioff and Southwick, 2004) or stakeholder capitalism; a model of capitalism that looks beyond shareholder value to embrace a variety of different social purposes and responsibilities towards stakeholders. It is a model of doing business that is indeed becoming increasingly popular and notable, for instance in the influential 2019 Davos manifesto. Representing some of the world's most powerful business leaders, the manifesto argues for a better kind of capitalism, one that directly tackles 'social and environmental challenges'.[3] Within the manifesto, stakeholder capitalism is contrasted not only with 'shareholder capitalism', a dominant Western model that believes a corporation's primary goal should be to maximise its profits, but also 'state capitalism', a model entrusting governments with directing the economy. The latter has risen to prominence in many emerging markets, not least China. Ultimately, whether stakeholder capitalism is sufficiently progressive depends on whether it proves to be primarily a rebranded form of current capitalism to save capitalism from itself, as opposed to saving the planet. It is also interesting that the Davos manifesto associates state capitalism exclusively with China, despite the other examples of welfare state economies that emerged after World War II across the so-called Western world, as well as the more contemporary welfare economies of Scandinavian Europe. State capitalism, if understood as a model based on greater state interference in (and beyond) the workings of the market, comes in rather different shapes and sizes.

FEMME-, QUEER-, WOKEWASHING? THE GAP BETWEEN SAYING AND DOING

Are the new genres of femvertising, queer and woke advertising primarily a marketing trend or part (however small!) of a more serious and growing movement against patriarchy, racism and other forms of structural inequality? It is certainly true that the primary beneficiary of such advertisements remains the brands themselves. As Banet-Weiser (2018) puts it in the context of femvertising, the archetypal recipient is an individual consumer seeking empowerment through market-mediated choices. Feminist action is reduced to catchy slogans, social media likes and a few extra pounds spent in supermarket tills. Such symbolic gestures couldn't be further removed from the kind of collective and far-reaching activism needed to effectively address structural change. No wonder, then, hashtags such as #wokewashing #femmewashing and #pinkwashing (and more recently, #coronawashing and #carewashing; Chatzidakis et al., 2020) are consistently trending in social media and are also the subject of many news media articles. Writing for *The Guardian*, for instance, Owen Jones (2019) exposes how wokewashing feeds an illusion of social change: 'while advertising campaigns have demonstrably helped rake in billions of pounds for big corporates, there is no evidence any have significantly changed the world for the better'.

Academic studies on the authenticity of woke advertising often take a rather more complicated stance. Authentic 'brand activism' is possible, according to Vredenburg et al. (2020), when the (woke) marketing message, the corporation's purpose and values, and the prosocial corporate practice are aligned. Archetypal examples include: TOMS' 'buy-one-give-one' campaign; Ben & Jerry's activism; and Patagonia's approach to anti-consumption. For these authors the key seems to be optimal (in)congruence between brand and socio-political (woke) cause. From the outset, it seems reasonable to assume that some corporations are more genuine in their commitment to certain social and environmental causes than others. Underpinning such understandings of authentic versus inauthentic woke advertising, however, is the rather more implicit assumption that a certain model of stakeholder capitalism is possible and indeed desirable. For other scholars and social commentators, it is our current socio-economic system that needs to be radically redesigned, including the role and nature of the corporation within it. Corporations can only do better, for instance, when their raison d'être is no longer pure profit but also genuine social and environmental accountability – an aim that is more effectively achieved through more cooperative, participatory and employee-driven models of corporate practice and governance (Paranque and Willmott, 2014).

And yet, as we observe above, if representation matters, advertising plays a central role in both reproducing and disrupting a series of heteronormative assumptions and practices that are naturalised and normalised. Contemporary femvertising, including its more intersectional manifestations in queer and woke advertising, is rich with interventions and resignifications that have disrupted some repetitions of heteronormativity and racism, even if only to produce and reproduce further problematic stereotypes (Sobande, 2019). Ultimately, whether there is potential for genuine political interventions in this realm also intersects with the distinction between what we identify as representational versus socio-economic levels of understanding gender politics, and the question on how to combine them. Put differently, gender stubbornly remains a two-sided category, containing 'both an economic face that brings it within the ambit of redistribution and also a cultural face that brings it simultaneously within the ambit of recognition' (Fraser, 2009, p. 2).

In conclusion, it is fair to say that femvertising (as well as woke and queer advertising) does have a role to play, however controversial, in advancing 'difference-friendly' imaginaries and therefore disrupting hetero- and cis-normativity. Nevertheless, whether this kind of recognition politics can be meaningfully combined with economic (re)distribution is far more controversial. For proponents of Fraser's so-called 'perspectival dualism' – the idea that cultural and economic spheres are anything but disconnected – 'recognition reforms cannot succeed unless they are joined with struggles for redistribution. In short, no recognition without redistribution' (Fraser, 2009, p. 9). Can femvertising affect struggles of economic redistribution, even if only indirectly by enhancing the status of some gendered identities? Perhaps, but the ever-increasing popularity of terms such as femmewashing and queerwashing means that many people remain highly sceptical of corporations that do not put their money (e.g. equal pay policies) where their mouth is (e.g. femvertising campaigns).

It is also possible that advertising helps people divert from the social struggles that really matter. These hardly ever correlate with choosing between different brands of (feminist versus non-feminist) moisturiser or (queer versus cis) razor blades. In other words, contemporary advertising may work to further decouple the politics of difference from the politics of equality. Finally, it is worth noting that advertising remains highly eclectic in terms of the politics of difference with which it engages. In other words, advertising is primarily focused on socio-demographic segments that, even if misunderstood or misrecognised, have some purchasing power potential. So, although it may no longer be as colour/ gender blind as it used to be, advertising remains blind and, indeed, totally oblivious to many other markers of social discrimination and their various intersections. Not everyone has sufficient wealth to be empowered through their marketplace, even if this was a realistic possibility. And many would argue that genuine empowerment cannot, and should not, be marketised.

NOTES

1. The concept of hegemonic masculinity is recognised for its normative
    effects as Connell and Messerschmidt (2005, p. 832) explain: 'Hegemonic
    masculinity was distinguished from other masculinities, especially subordi-
    nated masculinities. Hegemonic masculinity was not assumed to be normal
    in the statistical sense; only a minority of men might enact it. But it was
    certainly normative. It embodied the currently most honored way of being
    a man, it required all other men to position themselves in relation to it, and
    it ideologically legitimated the global subordination of women to men.'
2. See for example: https://medium.com/swlh/are-you-woking-why-brands-are
    -so-obsessed-with-woke-advertising-9852d3bedc94
3. https://www.weforum.org/agenda/2019/12/why-we-need-the-davos
    -manifesto-for-better-kind-of-capitalism/

4. Gendering products and services: from design to brand

Gendering products and services is one of the fundamental aspects of market segmentation, targeting and positioning – processes at the heart of strategic marketing. Marketers – in conjunction with product designers – frequently make gendered assumptions about users and the meanings they attach to products. For evidence of this we need look no further than the case of Marlboro cigarettes, a brand that dates back to 1924 – a time when it sought to tap into the then underdeveloped female market. Later, however, Marlboro repositioned the brand as masculine using the infamous rugged and macho Marlboro cowboy. Another, lesser-known example is the microwave oven, originally designed as a 'brown good' for heating prepared meals and targeted at young male users reluctant to waste time on meal preparation. User instructions accordingly conveyed the complexity associated with high-tech and it was sold in brown goods outlets alongside video recorders and stereo systems. When this initial positioning failed to achieve the anticipated market success, the microwave was revamped as a 'white good' with more extensive cooking facilities, including roasting and grilling. Then, as a family item, the presumption was that women would be the main users and, consequently, its high-tech programming was replaced by simpler pictograms to denote user possibilities. Distribution also changed and the microwave was sold, as it still is today, alongside other white goods such as cookers and refrigerators (Cockburn and Ormrod, 1993; Oudshoorn, Saetnan and Lie, 2002). Thus, the 'gender' of the microwave oven altered in terms of its targeted users, how and where it was sold and even in terms of its user instructions. As such, the development of the microwave exemplifies the ways designers and marketers make assumptions about potential users and the meanings they will attach to the product.

In this chapter we take a closer look at the gendering of products and services in tandem with considering the intersection of new technologies and marketing, both offline and online.

Of course, technology in general is an especially gendered field and the unequal gender relations that shape its design and development have long been documented (Cockburn and Omrod, 1993). This carries over to the online environment where a misogynistic culture and discourses in male-dominated internet communities alongside the pornification of culture have also been well documented (Jeong and Lee, 2018).

FEMINISM AND TECHNOLOGY: AN HISTORIC OVERVIEW

Initially feminist work in this area focused on the impact of technology in the home and at work, often portraying women as the passive victims of technology, which was seen as embodying patriarchal and capitalist interests (Lubar, 1998; Wajcman, 2000). Stemming from modernist assumptions that separated the public and private spheres, the design of technology was associated with the former (i.e. production, men and masculinity) whereas the use of technology was associated with the latter (i.e. consumption, women and femininity). The end of the 1980s marked a shift in emphasis towards a more complex view of the relationship between technology and gender. Consequently, studies examining how technologies are developed and used began to explore multi-user groups (web designers, product engineers, users, etc.) and their differing inter-pretations and understandings. At the same time, Butler's (1990) theories were beginning to influence the conceptualisation of gender as performa-tive and being constructed in social interaction. As a result, studies began to emphasise 'a two-way mutually shaping relationship between gender and technology in which technology is both a source and consequence of gender relations and vice-versa' (Faulkner, 2001, p. 81).

To consider this more closely, it is worth spending a moment to explore definitions of technology because, as a word, it is often misun-derstood. Its etymology lies in the ancient Greek τέχνη, techne, meaning 'art, skill, craft'. The *Oxford English Dictionary* defines it as: 'scientific knowledge used in practical ways in industry, for example in designing new machines'. Technology is thus associated with physical objects whose materiality can have a very embodied influence on human activ-ity. As such, technology can be thought of as a 'system comprised of artifacts, social practices and systems of knowledge' (Fox, Johnson and Rosser, 2006, p. 2). Gender and technology are intricately entwined with one affecting the other, a process that Fox, Johnson and Rosser (2006) refer to as their 'co-creation thesis'. So, for example, we tend to find that often traditional divisions of labour within a household apply: men look after those tasks involving technology (cars, DIY, cutting hedges, mowing the grass, etc.) whereas women take care of what are deemed to be non-technical tasks (childminding, cooking and cleaning). Yet pans, pots, cleaning equipment and childcare are also systems of knowledge. This, then, begs the question whether the gendered division of household duties is caused by the association of masculinity with technology or whether stereotypical gender relations lead to tasks being classified as either technological or non-technological. According to Fox, Johnson and Rosser (2006) their co-creation model provides a way to unpack the complexities of the two-way relationship with technology, i.e gender affecting technology and technology affecting gender.

Unpacking these relationships more, it is also useful to understand the interlinked aspects of structures, gender symbols and identities. In relation to structural aspects, strong divisions of labour around technology exist both in its production and consumption (Wajcman, 2000; Faulkner, 2001). As we illustrated at the outset, the consumption of technology is often gendered by association, as evidenced in the gendered division of household technologies. White goods that bear the brunt of routine domestic tasks (washing machines, dishwashers, etc.) are likely to be associated with femaleness, whereas technologies used for DIY tasks such as power drills as well as black/brown goods (music systems, televisons, etc.) are more associated with maleness.

When it comes to the production side, there are comparatively fewer studies of the gender–technology relationship because women are less likely to be involved in the innovation and design stages of technological developments (although they are, of course, involved as production workers). Product engineers tend to be male and to consider housework technology to be rather basic and undemanding, whereas leisure and entertainment technology is seen as more challenging and creative (Cockburn, 1997). In relation to the aforementioned microwave oven, it was designed by male engineers with female input limited to the contribution of home economists who advised on consumer aspects (Cockburn and Ormrod, 1993). Yet, engineers devalued the technical skills of these women, thus limiting their influence on the microwave's design.

Gender symbolism also makes a significant contribution to making technologies a male domain because often technologies may incorporate symbols, metaphors and values that have masculine connotations (Rommes, Van Osst and Oudshoorn, 2001). Indeed, it has been well documented how low-tech areas such as household technologies are more likely to stress hegemonic feminine values such as care and user-friendliness whereas high-tech areas such as space technologies emphasise hegemonic masculine values such as the power of humankind to control the universe (Pacey, 1983). As a result, features can be designed into technologies that reflect and reinforce gender stereotypes (Faulkner, 2001) as in our opening example of the microwave oven which showed how this 'symbolic' gendering of technology can also have material effects (complexity of use etc).

GEEK CULTURE: THE DEFAULT MALE IN PRODUCT DESIGN

Despite the fact that many women are technically highly capable and many men are not, the image of technology as a male domain persists, seen as integral to the construction of masculinity, a point noted two decades ago by Wajcman (2000) but one that still remains relevant today. Indeed, research has shown the pleasure male engineers find in working with technologies and how this plays a key element in their sense of individual and professional identities, whereas their female counterparts did not share the same obsession with technology (McIlwee and Robinson, 1992). In her book, *Pleasure, Power and Technology*, Sally Hacker (1989) insightfully reveals how the pleasures of making things work can turn into processes of domination. To this end, she exposes the links between gender, technology and military institutions. But even in the everyday workplace, technical expertise may be used as a type of symbolic power by those with relatively little other power, either in terms of class or professional standing (Downey and Lucena, 1995). Similarly, this quest for power and control through technological expertise is equally relevant in the online environment, as applicable to computer hacking as it is to computer programming, both male dominated areas (Faulkner, 2001; Adam, 2003).

Yet, it is important to emphasise that 'geek culture' does not exclude all women and nor is computer science always coded masculine. In other words, the assumptions that underpin hegemonic Western masculinity cannot be just assumed to be universally applicable (Wajcman, 2010). Consider Malaysia, for example, where there are many female computer scientists and where the discipline is not strongly associated with masculinity per se (Lagesen, 2008). There, computer science is perceived as appropriate for women because of its associations with office work, a space generally regarded as safer than other areas of technology such as construction sites or factories.

Moreover, although computer hacking has traditionally been conceived as a male arena with little female participation, in the last decade there has been an emergence of feminist hackerspaces, namely online spaces that are women-centred and guided by feminist principles (Toupin, 2014). These challenge the open space model of male-dominated hackerspaces in offering safe spaces for marginalised identities, spaces where political resistance can take place as well.

Given this deep-rooted dominance of technology by men, it is scarcely surprising to learn that the world is designed for men, as writer and activist, Caroline Criado Perez, contends in her book, *Invisible Women* (2019). The failure to include women's perspectives sufficiently in the design process often leads to unintended male biases in product design and Criado Perez presents us with some frightening consequences. One shocking fact, for example, is that cars are designed around a male body and, consequently, women are nearly 50 per cent more likely to be seriously hurt than men in collisions. This, despite the fact that men are more likely to crash!

In what Criado Perez (p. 3) describes as a 'male-unless-otherwise-indicated' approach, designers of technology, and even scientists more broadly, presume a default male at the heart of their studies. As a result, the generic masculine permeates everything from language itself ('mankind') to historical figures on banknotes,[1] top film roles and even children's non-human TV characters. Smartphones and piano keyboards too big for the average woman's handspan, smartwatches that don't fit women's wrists and Google's voice recognition technology 70 per cent more likely to recognise a male voice – the list is endless. From augmented reality glasses to the Fitbit's calculations of movement, Criado Perez sets out a copious catalogue of product and technology design and development underpinned by gendered data.

MARKETING HIS AND HERS

But what is marketing's role in all this? Marketers have long been acknowledged as the translators between production and consumption, between the public sphere of (men's) work and the private sphere of domesticity. As to the latter, the relationship between femininity and consumption – with its many seductive temptations – has been an enduring one from the mid-19th century onwards; a period when consumer agency shifted from male to female in American consumer culture (Witkowski, 2017). Thus marketing, unlike other disciplines, has always been interested in the female consumer, the *she* that was taken for granted in early marketing and consumer behaviour texts (Frederick, 1929). Marketing researchers validated topics that explored the minutiae of women's everyday lives long before sociologists took an interest. The study of meal preparations, washing clothes and other household management tasks provided endless sources of inspiration in the search for new market opportunities. Despite this preoccupation with female concerns, marketers do not appear to have played any role in exposing the inherent masculine biases just discussed. We have already mentioned how home economists, responsible for the introduction of much technology in the home, were not welcomed in design processes either. It seems, therefore, that marketers, like the home economists in the early half of the 20th century, are more likely to be associated with the 'saleable' aspects of goods once their technological functions are completed, namely the aesthetics, the benefits offered and, of course, the symbolic meanings thereby conferred.

A useful entrée to understanding marketing's role in how different gender realities are reflected and reproduced within the sphere of consumption is to focus on the symbolic aspects of possessions and the social interactions they facilitate. The notion of the 'augmented product' (Levitt, 1980) looms large in consumer research, separating a product's material effects from its more symbolic ones. The implication is that, apart from the core product (primary benefit or reason for its purchase) and the actual product (the delivery of this benefit), there are additional 'augmented' features that often relate to more intangible, symbolic aspects such as aesthetic satisfaction, perceived desirability, ethicality, and so on (Chatzidakis and Maclaran, 2020). From this perspective, the perceived gender of an object or activity becomes an additional 'augmented' benefit that reinforces a consumer's 'gender identity congruity' (Oakenfull, 2012). Such processes were very evident in our discussions of the microwave oven and the Marlboro brand.

Another revealing example is the radio and how it too crossed gender boundaries. Initially aimed at male hobbyists as the 'wireless', it was promoted as a scientific, modern technology to enable 'geeks' to demonstrate their technical prowess, finding distant stations in their garages or attics (Lubar, 1998). At this stage, as a piece of very complex but functional equipment, it was basically just an ugly box. Yet, although the radio's audience was mainly male, the market for its advertising was primarily female consumers. This meant that women had to want it in the home and, hence, the aesthetics of the box were improved to enable the radio to fit in with domestic interior decors, making it more like a piece of furniture. Marketers then promoted it as a family product that could enhance domesticity and family life.

Of course, it's not always marketers or designers who dictate all the meanings of a product or service and sometimes initial meanings can be reinterpreted as users interact with a particular technology. A well-known example of this is the early marketing of the telephone in the 1900s ' and how it was originally envisaged as a business tool – the domestic connection was merely to ensure that businessmen could be contacted at home. Although it was not foreseen, women used home telephones to chat to friends and family. Eventually the telephone companies realised that it was more profitable to charge for the duration of the call rather than the connection made (Rakow, 1992). Yet, associations of the telephone as masculine persisted for nearly a century in conjunction with the wide disparagement of female use of the phone as frivolous. British Telecommunications turned all this on its head with their iconic 'It's Good to Talk' campaign in the 1990s. Underpinning this innovative, and highly successful, approach was culturally orientated marketing research that identified the gendered perceptions of telephone usage (Alexander, Burt and Collinson, 1995). 'Big Talk' was masculine, information focused and serious, whereas its feminine counterpart, 'Small Talk', was perceived as trivial and unimportant. The clever campaign that resulted from this research emphasised the many emotional benefits of seemingly purposeless social interactions. Fronted by the much-loved actor Bob Hoskins each advertisement unveiled problematic, everyday situations that were solved because of social bonds cemented through regular communications. More recently in 2017, BT has harked back to this message in a brand strategy that emphasises 'Be There', a strategy that runs across its various offerings (BT Infinity, BT Sport, B2B activities) and one that emphasises human relationships and closeness.

In the main, however, it is fair to say that marketers, in treating gender as a key demographic variable in market segmentation, have often contributed to gender stereotyping in developing new products and services, either by emphasising or constructing gender differences rather than similarities. Nowhere is this more acute than in relation to the children's toy and clothing markets where pink for girls and blue for boys is very much a given in Western countries. The blame for these colour preferences lies fairly and squarely with marketers who from the 1950s onwards sought new (and easy) market opportunities. After all, such colour coding makes it more difficult to share clothes and toys between sons and daughters, thereby driving increased purchasing behaviours and growing markets. The fact that a century ago pink was more likely to be associated with boys and masculinity highlights the culturally constructed nature of these gender differences on the basis of colour. Indeed, advice issued by *Earnshaw's Infants' Department*, in 1918 leaves us in no doubt: 'The generally accepted rule is pink for the boys, and blue for the girls. The reason is that pink, being a more decided and stronger color, is more suitable for the boy, while blue, which is more delicate and dainty, is prettier for the girl' (Paoletti, 2012).

Beyond children's markets, marketers sometimes use blue as a masculine cue on packaging or brand logos to signify competence whereas pink colours cue femininity and can be used to denote compassion. Shapes are also often used as gender cues – round for female and angular for male. However, sometimes gender coding can have an adverse effect, especially if a product is perceived as too masculine or too feminine. Research on the 'Pink Ribbon' breast cancer campaign showed that the use of pink diminished the campaign's effectiveness because by associating the colour with themselves women subconsciously experienced denial (Puntoni et al., 2011). Another study revealed that in the case of reputable brands perceived as highly competent, feminine cues can lend more warmth and increase purchase likelihood, while this likelihood decreased with masculine cues (Hess and Melnyk, 2016). Following this logic, we can understand why Apple (a highly reputable/competent brand) chose to feature a pink flower on the release of its iPhone 6. Conversely, whenever there are low competence associations such as with a new product launch or business start-up, masculine cues can enhance purchase intentions.

It is important to recognise that such gendering of services and products by marketers often directly perpetuates gender-related injustices. An obvious manifestation is the so-called 'gender surcharge' and/or 'pink tax'. These colloquial terms reflect the well-known observation that women's products are often more expensive. A 2016 investigation by *The Times*, for instance, found that women are being charged, on average, 36 per cent more for products marketed as 'women's' (BBC News, 2016). Oftentimes the only existing reason for a price difference, from razor blades to children's scooters, is their colour; that is, pink versus blue. Accordingly, groups of MPs and consumer organisations have often mobilised against such unfair pricing.

Another way in which the gendering of services and products perpetuates social injustices is by limiting the choices and interests of people on the basis of their gender. As noted above, most toy retailers and manufacturers market toys for girls and boys separately. Action, construction and science toys are more commonly marketed to boys whereas role play, arts and crafts are commonly targeting girls. Research conducted by Let Toys be Toys,[2] a UK-based consumer advocacy and market research group, found that UK TV channels consistently portray boys as 'active and aggressive', with adverts emphasising 'power, control and conflict'.[3] In contrast, girls are portrayed as 'passive, unless they were dancing', with adverts focusing on themes such as fantasy, relationships and beauty. Accordingly, the campaign by Let Toys be Toys asks retailers and marketers to ditch gender stereotypes and market their products by theme and function rather than gender. Interestingly, beyond the question of gender justice, the campaign also points to the detrimental effects that gender stereotyping has for the environment, given that families (and broader communities) with both boys and girls have fewer toys to hand down from one child to another.

Of course, it is not just toys that are notoriously gendered and non-inclusive. There are numerous other examples of how marketers limit consumers' product choices and experiences on the basis of fixed gender tropes and stereotypes. Many retail environments continue to be heavily gendered, limiting access to visitors and customers that do not conform to the targeted gender profile. Consider that until relatively recently, men's personal care products such as under-eye and serum creams could only be found at speciality stores. Now they are healthily represented in most major department stores or supermarkets (Chatterjee and Monroe, 2020).

GENDER-NEUTRAL MARKETING

Despite the observation that many marketers continue to leverage gender cues strategically and tactically in developing markets and positioning products and services, we are now seeing much wider public awareness of the role this plays in gender stereotyping. Gender-neutral marketing has emerged as a response to biting criticisms from consumer campaign groups, such as Let Toys be Toys mentioned above, but also market research showing GenZ consumers value brands that do not classify items as male or female (Francis and Hoefel, 2018), and nor do young parents when it comes to choosing services and products for their children (Powers, 2019). Reflecting these trends, LEGO has recently launched a LGBTQI+ set titled 'everyone is awesome'. Out of the 11 new minifigures only one has a specific gender, that is a purple minifigure with a highly stylised wig which clearly references drag queens. The rest of the minifigures have no specific gender although their colours reflect the LGBTQI+ flag. They are meant to 'express individuality, while remaining ambiguous' (Russell, 2021). Other notable examples include Diet Coke's 2019 Super Bowl advertisement that runs with the tagline 'There's a Coke for he and she and her and me and them. There's a different Coke for all of us'; and Samuel Adams Boston Lager's explicit attempt to downplay masculine associations in its redesigned packaging.

The enthusiastic embrace of gender-neutral marketing by many household brands can also be explained rather more cynically as part of the realm of wokewashing (discussed in the previous chapter), or as an attempt to redress reputational damages of previously gendered campaigns. BIC, for instance recently introduced a 'Made for You' razor blade that is marketed as gender-inclusive, that is for 'whoever you are, wherever you shave … It is not just the best razor for men, it is not just the best razor for women, we make the best razor for everybody.'[4] A few years earlier, the same company was in the spotlight for one of the most ridiculed examples of gendered marketing, that is a Bic pen 'For Her' that was 'designed to fit comfortably into a woman's hand' and which was priced 70 per cent higher than the classic, non-gendered pen.

Gender-neutral marketing is also increasingly prevalent in the services sector, not least in the self-care and beauty industries, from beauty spas to hairdressers. London's and Prague's 'Open Barbers' is a very successful hairdressing service for 'all lengths, genders and sexualities' that has been running for more than ten years.[5] The salon offers a queer and trans friendly attitude, with many of the hairdressers (and the customers) identifying as such and opting for haircuts that do not follow 'gender appropriate' conventions. Interestingly, the salon also runs a safe social space and has a sliding scale pricing policy, which means that customers are asked to pay what they can, in accordance with their means, thereby also acknowledging the intersectional nature of gender ideology.

More generally, the self-care and fashion industries are increasingly embracing gender neutrality. Browns East, a luxury fashion store in East London, follows 'a gender-neutral approach, the entire flexible space combines womenswear and menswear collections from the finest names in luxury with the tastemakers of tomorrow'.[6] May other major spas, wellness centres and cosmetics retailers, such as Aesop or Ordinary, now adopt explicitly genderless product lines and store atmospherics. Similarly, store chains such as Target have stripped kids' toys and bedding sections of gender identifiers whereas Stockmann, Finland's largest department store, now has a floor dedicated to gender-neutral fashion.

The adoption of gender-neutral approaches in such sectors is perhaps not surprising. From a more managerialist approach, it is testament to the fact that gender neutrality sells more than product and service augmentations do based on rigid gender binaries. After all, other industries, from banking to legal and consultancy services, have long differentiated their offerings by function rather than gender. Hence, it is arguably the sectors traditionally offering more opportunities for symbolic display and differentiation that have largely relied on gender tropes – tropes now seen as increasingly dated, at least by some part of the population. Of course, the flip side is the co-optation of gender inclusivity to enhance profitability. Another contradiction, as we explain in Chapter 6, is that many forms of emotional and intimate labour, from call centre operators to flight attendants, continue to be largely devalued because of their systemic feminisation, even while (and regardless of whether) they cater for multiple genders.

THE GENDERING OF DIGITAL PRODUCTS AND SERVICES

Aside from growth in gender-neutral fashion, especially in digital retail spaces, and the well-documented gender fluidity of millennials (Jauk, 2018; Diamond, 2020), the online environment remains male dominated in many respects. It is therefore worth examining historically how this has come to pass. Indeed, the initial assumption was that the computer has no inherent gender bias. The early days of the internet were heralded as conferring freedom from biases based on the physical markers of gender, race, class and other social cues (Turkle, 1986; Herring, 1993). Yet, as already mentioned earlier in this chapter, it is now widely recognised that computer culture, as with other technologies, reproduces the same unequal power relations embedded in our institutional and cultural processes. Online interactions still consist of gendered discourses and practices that exist in the offline social and political contexts of participants' everyday lives (Southern and Harmer, 2021).

Undoubtedly, we can single out the markets for computer games as major contributory factors to male dominance of computer culture. From an early age, boys are socialised into the use of computers through the plethora of computer games that cater for their needs, encouraging competition and normalising violence (Maclaran et al., 2004). By contrast, few computer games are designed to appeal to girls and even an innocuous, but highly popular, computer game such as *Tomb Raider* reinforces stereotypical images of women, with its central character portrayed as a sex object complete with bursting bust line (Hocks, 1999). Although some girl-orientated software has been developed, this is often based on an essentialist assumption that girls and boys have different preferences and does nothing to challenge the assumptions that underpin traditional gender dichotomies. Harking back to our previous discussions on technology, different metaphors and representations alter possible readings in the software that children can make and, in turn, affect their performance with the software. Yates and Littleton (2001) conclude that the preferred readings of most computer games are orientated to male subject positions and cultural competencies. This is borne out by the fact that in the 15 or so years since Yates and Littleton's (2001) research – and despite the number of women gamers now being almost equal to those of male gamers – women still find it very difficult to be acknowledged as 'real gamers' in an industry that continues to be heavily associated with masculinity and many ongoing instances of female stigmatisation (Paaßen, Morgenroth and Stratemeyer, 2017). In their call for more research into the gendered nature of the gaming marketplace, Drenten, Harrison and Pendarvis (2019) stress the need for more understanding of consumers' lived experiences in this gendered subculture as well as more research that explores its systemic, structural and cultural biases.

As regards the internet more broadly, feminists have long highlighted how its origins were in the male worlds of the military, the academy, engineering and industry and how this accounts for the lessened participation of women and other minority groups. The persistence of sexism on the internet has been well documented (Bruckman, 1993; Spender, 1995). In her research on sites where interactive role-playing games take place, Kendall (1999) showed how such online environments may feel particularly foreign to women as they encounter a social atmosphere with behaviour patterns formed largely by men. The women participants in her study were regularly exposed to sexual harassment in the form of sexist jokes, rude comments and bullying. Although participants in role-playing games could choose their gender designation (male, female or gender neutral), this did not change the expectations that were attached to particular gender identifications. Thus, Kendall (1999) found that how male and female characters behave depended on wider cultural beliefs about feminine and masculine behaviours so that, even in innovative fantasy environments, standard expectations of masculinity and femininity tended to dominate. For this reason, female characters were more likely to be less valued than their male counterparts and, therefore, less likely to be chosen in the first place.

Turning to Mulvey's theory of the gaze, there is evidence of character representations following stereotypical body constructions of active/male and passive/female. According to White (2001, p. 143), these descriptions 'perpetuate the dominant cinema's scripting of male subjects who control and look upon female objects'. Even in relation to gender switching, the potential is more limited than originally anticipated by feminists such as Plant (1995). A research study on virtual fantasy worlds found that only a minority of players engaged in gender switching and more than half of those who did only did so for less than 10 per cent of their time online (Roberts and Parks, 2001). Furthermore, a majority of participants who switched genders kept within traditional gender binaries, ignoring the multiple gender-neutral categories offered. And, despite its strong feminist orientation, another fantasy website, 'Raising Men For Fun', an online dating game that reversed traditional Chinese male/female relationships, failed to sustain gender reversal for long (Chen, Davies and Elliott, 2002). Here women played the role of master and men played the role of their pet although there was also deceit sometimes when women played a male pet or men played a female master. The resultant anxieties were found to make the deceptions unsustainable in the long term. Now, of course, nearly 20 years later, the increasing normalisation of gender fluidity amongst the millennial generation is likely to assuage such anxieties by making such strict adherence to binary gender categories a redundant notion. Mainstream social networking sites currently offer a range of gender identity options; Facebook (UK) has over 70 definitions of gender and a popular dating app, Tinder, allows users to choose from 37 options.

Nevertheless, millennial acceptance of gender fluidity has still to make an impact on sexism on the internet, and more and more we find what Banet-Weiser and Miltner (2016) refer to as 'networked misogyny' proliferating on contemporary social media sites. These authors declare us to be 'in a new era of the gender wars, an era that is marked by alarming amounts of vitriol and violence directed toward women in online spaces' (p. 171). As they explain, this misogyny is also racist and frequently targets women of colour specifically. Often the anonymity of the internet is deemed the culprit for such behaviours as well as the masculine culture of technology and insufficient legal frameworks to regulate online practices. But according to Banet-Weiser and Miltner, this distracts from the fact that misogyny is deeply embedded in Western culture where it is naturalised in taken-for-granted power relations that bring about gender inequality in the first instance. A feminist interrogation of popular internet memes of online sexism showed how humour is frequently used to reframe online sexism as acceptable, thereby dismissing it as mere banter (Drakett et al., 2018). Often this sexism – reflecting heteronormative, hegemonic masculinity – uses irony and joking to police and regulate online spaces and to make others who are different feel they don't belong.

THE MARKET FOR PORNOGRAPHIC VIOLENCE AGAINST WOMEN

Nowhere is misogyny more pronounced than in the flourishing markets for fantasies of sexual violence that many pornography sites offer. The shift to digital technologies has greatly expanded pornography's reach and it now has a global market value of US$100 billion plus according to recent estimates (Anciaux, 2020). With its easy accessibility on smartphones, it has become a common form of harassment to degrade women both in public spaces and in the workplace (McVey, Gurrieri and Tyler, 2018). However, not all pornography is misogynistic and there are many sites serving the LGBTQI+ communities, as well as a growing number targeting women, that may be considered empowering for those consumers who wish to develop their own sexuality and pleasures. So, in agreement with authors such as Lynne Segal (1993) and Drucilla Cornel (2004) and contra anti-porn feminists such as Andrea Dworkin (1981) and Catharine MacKinnon (1987) we are not making a blanket condemnation of pornography here. Indeed, the feminist debate over the role of pornography has a very long history, encapsulated in terms such as 'feminist sex wars' (Ziv, 2015), and is underpinned by many distinct and complex arguments that we cannot do justice to here. As Cornel (2004, p. 151) puts it 'the split between feminists who have insisted on sexual exploration and the redefinition of sex itself, and those feminists who have sought to protect women from the imagined brutality of male sexuality' is perhaps the most recurring and largely unresolved one in the history of feminism.

For our purposes, however, it is useful to briefly introduce a distinction between the politics of the *production* of pornography, and the interrelated politics of *distribution* (i.e. legal attempts by some feminists to stop the distribution of pornography) and the politics of *consumption* of pornography. The politics of production involve the actual harm done to women involved in the production of pornography (Ziv, 2015). Although there is no doubt that the industry involves considerable abuse and exploitation of women, anti-antiporn feminists argue that the blanket view of all pornographic actors as victims that are coerced into pornography is equally problematic. The politics of consumption have to do with men's' use of pornography and its potential implications (Ziv, 2015). Anti-porn feminists argue that there is a clear link between pornography and the harm experienced by some women, as well as a broader link between pornography and the degradation of women's status. Using a range of theoretical arguments (e.g. on the differences between sexual fantasy and reality) and empirical research, anti-antiporn feminists question such linkages. More importantly perhaps, they take issue with anti-porn feminists' outright denial of the possibility of female emancipation through pornography (e.g. Ziv, 2015). Rather than censoring pornography, they advocate reappropriating pornography, through exploring and constructing a more diverse range of female and queer sexual agencies. In sum, as Ziv (2015) puts it, whereas anti-porn feminists focus on harm, anti-antiporn feminists focus on opportunities for the construction of more positive female and queer subjectivities.

However, there can be no doubt that amid the plethora of enticing sexual options sold online there is a striking glorification of what is, often, violence against women. Attempts to foreground women's sexual agency, at least within the marketing realm, remain fewer and far between. As McVey et al. (2018) argue, through the creation of women as products (as well as many other subordinate groups, often based on particular ethnicities), this violence is part of the structural subordination of women. These authors foreground how a woman's right to choose (to be a porn star, for example) masks whether men should have the right to demand that women are sold in this way. Once again, the discourse of choice, with its emphasis on the individual, detracts from acknowledging any collective responsibility for this commodification. Thus, by using discursive practices that normalise pornography, the more violent aspects of the industry are masked, both in terms of its production and consumption. For example, conflating the consumption of books like the *Fifty Shades* series with men's consumption of women is one such false equivalence (McVey et al., 2018).

As regards the production side of pornography, what Pezzutto (2019) terms 'porntrepreneurs' are leveraging social media to develop their own personal brands around differentiated erotic and sexual services. In response to radical transformations in the industry that have seen the demise of the traditional studio as the central workplace, performers are forced to become more self-reliant and follow a neoliberal market logic. Self-branding has therefore become vital to their success as they establish online personas to target particular groups of porn consumers with relevant material. The overall aim is to attract loyal followers and build an audience to monetise their social media brand (Pezzutto, 2019). Crucially, their success depends on how skilfully they can embody a particular fantasy, leading to a continual process of self-surveillance that can be emotionally draining. As they compare themselves to competitors and find themselves lacking in some respect, this process may result in surgical interventions to their physiques (breast augmentation, etc.). In her study of transgender porntropeneurs, Pezzutto reports many instances of body modifications and enhancements arising from the intense critical scrutiny to which their bodies are subjected. Added to this are the stalking, bullying and trolling behaviours the performers experience, animosities causing great stress and feelings of vulnerability that ultimately affect their mental health.

THE PORNIFICATION OF MARKETING AND THE MARKETING OF PORNOGRAPHY

The intertwining of the porn industry with mainstream culture is a major factor in its normalisation, one that marketers contribute to more widely, particularly in the fashion and music industries, as well as social media. Some of us may recall the infamous Dolce and Gabbana advertisement in 2007, banned shortly after its release (for offending the dignity of women), as proof of this point. Many believed the ad simulated gang rape when it showed a swimsuit clad model being pinned down by the wrists by a half-dressed man while his three friends looked on. This resonates with the comments of Ariel Levy, author of *Female Chauvinist Pigs: Women and the Rise of Raunch Culture* (2005), 'Sex sells. That's our justification for everything. The sex industry has become every industry' (cited in Penny, 2010, p. 5), with huge pressure on young women to create and maintain erotic capital. Alexandra Rome vividly documents the impact of this increasing eroticisation on young women's sexual subjectivities, revealing that, despite believing they are sexually empowered, there is an increasing internalisation of the 'women as abject' trope that reiterates patriarchal values (Rome, 2022). This abjectification seems to chime with journalist and activist, Laurie Penny's (2010, p. 11) words that sexual performance and self-objectification have become 'forms of work: duties that must be undertaken and perfected if we are to advance ourselves'. Citing the power of porn, she argues that young men and women are growing up with a distorted view of sex that is mechanical and, often, deeply misogynistic too.

Marketers feed the pornification of culture not only through the fashion and music systems, but also in positioning new markets such as pole dancing and burlesque as empowering choices for women (Dines, 2010). In a similar vein, there has been a glamorisation of bourgeois prostitution with TV programmes such as *The Secret Diary of a Call Girl* (TV series 2007–2011), a comedy featuring the sexual adventures of a high-class London escort with the working name Belle de Jour (otherwise Hannah) and played by Billie Piper.

The Playboy bunny is a well-loved and accepted logo that can be found on a vast swathe of fashion items that cover anything from socks to hoodies as well as children's stationery items and bedding. Such products reflect a growing trend for toys that have sexual overtones, such as Bratz dolls and even a child's bed with the brand name Lolita. And in 2018, the online fashion brand, Missguided, designed a range of clothing sporting the logo in collaboration with Playboy, making the emblem once again a fashion statement even though many people accused the brand of being 'tacky' and 'problematic' (Robinson, 2020).

The flipside of the pornification of marketing is the marketing of porn. Over the last two decades, various popular websites and 'porntropreneurs' (discussed above) have used both traditional and more creative forms of communication to reach wider audiences and normalise pornography. An emblematic example is Pornhub, now one of the world's most prominent websites that regularly features in the top 50 most-visited website lists, and which has unprecedentedly and notoriously engaged (or at least has tried to) with above-the-line advertising campaigns. These include a gigantic billboard in Times Square that was taken down a few hours later (Parkinson, 2014) and an attempt – declined by CBS – to air a short commercial during the American Super Bowl. More substantively, and being acutely aware of the challenges in negotiating space in more traditional marketing channels, Pornhub designed and executed a unique word-of-mouth and social media strategy that has been acclaimed across the business and marketing press (*Business Matters*, 2020). This largely relied on shareable (non-pornographic) content that featured numerous puns, alterations of existing internet memes, and witty jokes; all playing on the idea that everyone enjoys watching pornography and wastes too much time on it, yet hardly anyone feels comfortable talking about it. All Pornhub's social media channels are led by a fictional character called Aria, a girl next door who 'doesn't do porn' but stays up to date with everything going on in social media. Some examples of taglines used across Pornhub's media platforms are: 'Bad acting, terrible scripts. You will love it'; 'It's ok, you can touch yourself. #coronavirus', 'Making people delete their browsing history since 2007.' In addition, Pornhub's content marketing strategy relies on consistently sharing its data on viewing habits via its data-driven blog 'Insights', and through partnering with mainstream news and content sites such as Buzzfeed, Vice and Gizmondo.

Of course, the marketing savviness of the pornographic industry extends beyond marketing communications to encompass the entirety of the marketing mix. During the first serious COVID-19 wave witnessed in Italy, for instance, Pornhub offered its premium service for free to the entire population, a gesture that could be interpreted by some as corporate social responsibility or conversely, an example of corona-washing or carewashing (Chatzidakis et al., 2020). More simply still, it could be seen as creative price promotion. But this was not the first attempt by Pornhub to be a good corporate citizen. In relation to environmental justice, Pornhub famously launched a cause-related marketing campaign that included an adult video, titled 'the Dirtiest Porn Ever'. The video was filmed on a dirty beach where litter pickers wearing Pornhub uniforms are seen cleaning up the beach while a couple is having sex. Every time the video is played, Pornhub made a donation to 'Ocean Polymers', an NGO that works at collecting and reprocessing plastic from the sea. In the words of Corey Pricey, Pornhub's vice president, 'We are dirty here but that doesn't mean our beaches need to be' (Gorbatch, 2019).

In normalising porn advertising and attempting to be socially and environmentally responsible, Pornhub is a pioneer in the mainstreaming of pornography but is certainly not alone. CamSoda, a live streaming webcam platform, for instance, has offered free porn to all passengers who were quarantined on a COVID-hit cruise ship, and free cameras to players from the Kansas City chiefs and the San Franscisco 49ers in the lead up to Super Bowl LIV (Bien-Aimé, 2020), among others. For critics, the extensive use of such creative marketing strategies by porn industry actors is a problem potentially bigger than specific examples of pornifica-tion. It serves to glamorise and normalise an industry that is rampant with multiple forms of worker abuse and extreme exploitation. Put differently, it normalises rather than problematises both porn production and porn consumption. Whether at the same time it offers opportunities for the reappropriation of pornography and the construction of alternative sexual agencies remains a more complex question.

NOTES

1. Criado Perez led a successful campaign to reinstate a woman on British banknotes after Elizabeth Fry, a prison reformer, was replaced by Winston Churchill. From 2017 the image of Jane Austen appeared on the £10 note.
2. https://www.lettoysbetoys.org.uk/why-it-matters/
3. https://www.lettoysbetoys.org.uk/research/tv-advertising-research/
4. http://www.wearemadeforyou.com/
5. https://openbarbers.com/
6. https://www.brownsfashion.com/uk/boutique/browns-east

5. Marketing's free externalities: the well-being of human and non-human others

The pursuit of self-interest is deeply embedded in the logic of free market economies. It is scarcely surprising, therefore, that the environment receives little recognition in marketing practice. After all, market-less resources are accorded little worth by an economic ideology that leaves self-directed market forces to determine resource allocation. Consequently, and despite claims to the contrary (see our earlier discussion of 'greenwashing'), marketers largely treat environmental issues as externalities beyond their control and use the environment as a 'free' resource. To illustrate, consider the costings for long-haul transport: these are normally things like fuel, labour and vehicle investment, costings that typically ignore the cost of environmental pollution caused. Such a viewpoint conceptualises nature as serving mankind, reflecting a long-standing dominant social paradigm (DSP) rooted in androcentrism, a patriarchal worldview that is to blame for the heightened destruction of the environment we are currently witnessing. Marketing's treatment of the environment thus becomes a gendered problem because the natural world has traditionally been associated with the feminine, the creation of life and the nurturing position this implies.

Like the environment, care work and all the labour that is necessary for the sustenance of human lives is another externality that does not get properly valued. Many feminist scholars and activists have long pointed out that the realm of social reproduction has been structurally invisibilised, gendered and racialised with a view to support mainstream economic 'production' at the lowest cost possible. Therefore, the work that, for example, many (primarily) women do in the home in support of their children's upbringing, or the care provided to the elderly, remains either nonpaid or underpaid, while at a cultural level it is not recognised as being as significant as the work that (primarily) men undertake in the formal economy. In the second part of this chapter, we consider the more specific role that markets and marketing play in supporting and normalising the current status quo.

This chapter explores these free externalities and their gendered nature in more detail. First, we discuss more about the DSP and tackle its patriarchal logics from an ecofeminist perspective, both ideologically and in practice, with an illustrative case study of its principles applied to goddess culture in Glastonbury. Then we broaden our discussions to consider how the ideology of free markets and consumerism has begun to interpenetrate realms of care provision that have been traditionally driven by non-market values and logics, including the family but also communities and the support provided by states. In doing so, and contrary to the more feminine caring subject that is cultivated in places such as Glastonbury, the ideology of consumerism encourages modes of subjectivity that are increasingly instrumental, individualist and unwilling to extend their care across difference and distance. Subsequently, we consider the role that marketing communications play in portraying and legitimising corporations as institutions that care for people and the planet. We engage with the more recent notion of 'carewashing' (The Care Collective, 2020), a term referring to corporate attempts to describe themselves as caring while strategically distracting from activities that are socially and environmentally harmful. Altogether then, this chapter considers some of the main critiques of marketing, both as an institution and an industry that is complicit in undermining more transformative modes of collective well-being and care provision for *both* people and the planet.

THE DOMINANT SOCIAL PARADIGM

The DSP comprises the values, beliefs, norms and institutions that give meaning to our political and social worlds. Significantly, its legitimisation depends on reinforcement by a society's dominant groups and it acts like ideology, becoming a template for social and political action (Kilbourne, Beckmann and Thelen, 2002). As such, the DSP is a hidden driving force behind many taken-for-granteds embedded in institutional functions, as well as our everyday actions. Take, for example, the overriding quest for economic growth propelling endless consumerism, or the prerequisite for technological advancement that depletes natural resources faster than they can be replenished. Such givens – key principles of our current DSP – stem from European Enlightenment thinking of the 17th and 18th centuries that emphasises progress, freedom of the individual and dedication to reason and science. Although postmodernism has seriously critiqued the Enlightenment's master narratives, the latter's legacies still pervade much contemporary decision-making and attitude formation. One such legacy has been nature's long-standing association with chaos, as something that needs to be tamed and controlled by humankind for civilised society to thrive. Importantly too, the extent to which individuals believe in the DSP principles of economic and political liberation (i.e. free market capitalism) affects how much they are concerned about their role in environmental destruction. Strong believers in the DSP are likely to think that legislation or technology will solve any problems, rather than changing their own behaviours (Kilbourne, Beckmann and Thelen, 2002).

So, in its belief that humans are superior to and separate from the rest of nature, the DSP is anthropocentric rather that ecocentric, a worldview that recognises the interconnectedness of all the earth's living and non-living systems. Fundamentally, the anthropocentric essence of the DSP reflects the Enlightenment's nature–culture dualistic thinking, a highly gendered system of binary oppositions that positions the feminine/female on the side of nature (and body/emotion) against the more highly valued masculine/male associations of culture (and mind/reason). The section that follows will examine these logics more fully as we discuss the relevance of ecofeminism, a leading body of intellectual critique that brings together feminism and environmentalism.

ECOFEMINISM

Ecofeminism challenges dualistic thinking that privileges a masculine worldview and aligns the feminine with nature, creating both as 'other', a concept developed by Simone de Beauvoir to explain the hierarchical workings of the male-female gender binary and its implicit inequality (de Beauvoir, 1949). French feminist, Françoise d'Eaubonne (1994) is credited with first using the term ecofeminism in her work that linked the patriarchal domination of women as reproductive bodies to the overall domination and degradation of nature. Her critique of a biological determinism that positioned women as 'naturally' more in tune with the body and nature challenged binary systems of thought devaluing the feminine (Maclaran and Stevens, 2019). And, although various strands of ecofeminism have emerged over the years (i.e. social/Marxist ecofemism, cultural/spiritual ecofeminism and vegetarian ecofeminism) since d'Eaubonne's initial writings, they all agree on the close relationship between feminism and ecology (Warren, 2000). Another broad point of agreement between ecofeminists is the interconnectedness of all living things and the need to respect and reinstate nature as humankind's equal. From this perspective, the focus on a sense of self as separate in Western culture becomes a barrier to achieving this aim because individualism encourages a lack of responsibility or care towards others and, more generally, the world around us. A guiding principle of ecofeminist thinking is, therefore, to challenge such a 'self-other disjunction' (Gaard, 1993, p. 3) by striving to replace an androcentric and anthropocentric self with an ecological and interconnected self.

This conscious positioning of women with nature has led to harsh critiques of ecofeminism on the grounds of an essentialism[1] that places women in 'romanticized servitude' to nature (Ruether, 1975). Although a key aim of ecofeminists has been to challenge the dualism that links women to nature, it remains difficult for the movement to avoid conveying the notion that women are somehow closer to nature than men, particularly in relation to their embodied experiences, both biological and spiritual. Because of the essentialist tightrope that ecofeminists tread, many feminists avoid the term altogether, even if working at the intersection of feminism and the environment (Moore, 2015). For some, ecofeminism does not offer a new perspective and simply echoes cultural feminism as well as reinforcing patriarchal views of femininity. And Lucy Sargisson (2001, p. 52) has even gone so far as to describe it as 'the fluffy face of feminism'. Yet, the main contentions by ecofeminists – that other feminisms do not adequately address the gendered aspects of our treatment of the environment, and that the domination of both nature and women are closely interlinked – are not necessarily essentialist arguments in themselves.

However, a way to move forward from these recurrent debates, as Sargisson (2001, p. 54) suggests, is to regard ecofeminism as opening up a utopian space for 'transformative opposition' to core values embedded in a capitalist economy. At the same time, she warns that this utopianism should resist closure in envisaging a utopian blueprint that offers a vision of perfection. Such visions are the dark side of utopian thinking that replaces an ongoing critical and subversive challenging with totalitarianism (i.e. visions of a matriarchal society to replace a patriarchal one). Part of ecofeminism's utopian process, therefore, is creative and playful dreaming reflected in texts whose form and style disrupt academic norms. Here, Sargisson cites American author and activist, Starhawk, and her poetic texts elaborating her vision of an earth-based spirituality – a spirituality that Starhawk identifies as lacking in contemporary politics. At the forefront of the 1970s pagan spiritual revival, Starhawk is a prominent ecofeminist who co-founded Reclaiming, an activist movement combining contemporary witchcraft with environmentalism to create an inclusive neo-pagan spirituality. Her most famous work, *The Spiral Dance: A Rebirth of the Ancient Religion of the Great Goddess* (1979), is a classic of its genre (pagan spirituality). Giving an historical overview of the re-emergence of the Wicca religion, Starhawk details how Wicca's ancient practices can be adapted for the present day. As such, this work has become an important spiritual guidebook challenging the spiritual supremacy of patriarchal figures and the overriding masculine image associated with religious leaders. At the heart of these practices lies worship of the goddess, conceived as immanent in the Earth's cycles of birth, growth, death, decay and regeneration. From this perspective, each person embodies the divine. These are central tenets of the Reclaiming tradition, a movement that links commitment to nature with political action to achieve nature's protection. Having originated in the San Francisco Bay area, Reclaiming communities can now be found across the US, Canada, Europe and Australia. Indeed, one of the present authors (Pauline) attended one of Reclaiming's periodic events to bring community members together where she joined in a spiral dance led by Starhawk. The 'Witchcamp' took place over five days in Glastonbury, the centre for spiritual tourism in England (see, for example, Scott and Maclaran, 2012). We will return to the marketplace for paganism and its intersection with the environment later in this chapter. First, however, we explore more thoroughly how ecofeminism has been used to date in offering critiques of marketing's relationship with nature.

ECOFEMINIST CRITIQUE IN MARKETING

Susan Dobscha initiated ecofeminist critique in marketing as far back as 1993, when she proposed a research agenda on environmentally related consumption. Her insightful analysis of marketing discourse reveals how responsibility for saving the environment is devolved to consumers at a micro, individual level and their decisions to buy environmentally friendly products. This devolution detracts from any more collective action to bring about change at a structural level. In addition, marketing discourse upholds cultural and social dualisms that place women in the role of 'angel in the ecosystem' (Plumwood, 1993, p. 9) and gives them sole responsibility for saving the planet, a position reaffirmed by McDonagh and Prothero (1997) in their critique of marketing's anti-ecological practices. Nonetheless, later work exposes how marketers also position nature as the enemy when it suits them, especially in relation to women's consumption of feminine hygiene, household cleaning and beauty products (Dobscha and Ozanne, 2000). Living an ecological life can challenge these marketing practices and can be a force for social change, as Dobscha and Ozanne (2001) argue in a subsequent study that focuses on an environmental action group. Echoing key ecofeminist principles, they underline how the concept of a self-in-relation-to-nature (citizen-as-conserver) rather than an individualistic self, can help overturn the DSP and lead to marketing and consumption practices that are more in harmony with the natural world.

Most recently, Dobscha and Prothero (2022) take on the war metaphor in marketing as they again use an ecofeminist perspective to address the climate crisis. They compare and contrast the different messaging strategies of two activist groups, World War Zero and Extinction Rebellion. Then, applying ecofeminist theory, they illuminate the neoliberal ideology underpinning the war metaphors employed by the former group in its communications emphasising competition as a battleground. Framing climate crisis as war perpetuates a patriarchal mindset which reinforces not only the DSP but also the narrative that women need saving (by large [male] corporations) – even while it erases women's unpaid labour. As an alternative to this way of thinking, Extinction Rebellion's use of ecofeminist ideals mean shared visions of the future that avoid blame and seek consensus in a bottom-up, grassroots participatory style.

A crucial part of living in harmony with the natural world depends on respect for the animal kingdom and ecofeminist perspectives have forcefully critiqued marketers' use of anthropomorphic images in advertising. For example, one study reveals how such humanised images, often designed to be comical, disconnect them from nature in rather abject and humiliating ways (Stevens, Kearney and Maclaran, 2013). Similarly, a follow-up study on brand mascots exposes the vested interests of the dairy industry (Stevens, Maclaran and Kearney, 2014). Featuring the tale of Elsie the Borden Cow from her creation in 1932 to the present day, this analysis reveals an overarching conceptual metaphor of benevolent mastery in relation to Elsie. In depicting man as a 'concerned and caring custodian' (p. 115), the metaphor points to the term 'animal husbandry' as symptomatic of this androcentric and anthropocentric perspective. Accordingly, the findings expose how humans are positioned as 'rational stewards' managing and controlling nature for its own best interests (Plumwood, 1993, p. 16). So the tale of Elsie, and her use as a brand mascot to produce an emotional response in consumers, provides an excellent example of the DSP in Western industrial societies. As discussed earlier, this permeates our social, cultural, political, economic and technological practices, setting humans apart from the natural environment and placing them in a privileged position over nature.

Apart from the dairy industry, ecofeminist analyses have also proved effective in putting tourism practices and the use of animals under the microscope. There are many ways that animals underpin tourism activities (Fennell, 2012): to be gazed upon in both wild habitats (safaris) and captive settings (circuses, zoos); used as transport (riding, pulling carriages and trailers); for public spectacles (bull fighting, greyhound racing, rodeos); and for sporting events (hunting, polo). Often the animals for such activities are kept in deplorable conditions, as are the animals used as food sources, another major factor in the tourism experience (Fennell, 2015). Indeed, as these authors highlight, food tourism is a growth area, especially given the contemporary experience economy fuelling the tourist quest for more embodied and sensory involvement in the contexts they are visiting. Exotic animals and their body parts on the menu are frequently used to give restaurants their competitive edges. Such commodification of animals, and its resultant market value sustaining the tourism industry, remain significant barriers to adopting more ethical relationships with animals who are very much treated as other-than-human. From an ecofeminist perspective, Fennell (2015) calls for more sustainable and 'morally defensible' (p. 66) approaches to animal welfare, approaches that reinstate the natural world's value eroded by the DSP.

We continue this theme of tourism in the next section, but with a change of emphasis as we present a case study of spiritual tourism guided by ecofeminist principles. Turning to the thriving marketplace for goddess culture in Glastonbury, England, we consider the spiritual and physical well-being it advocates through connectedness with the natural world and caring for the environment.

SELLING THE GODDESS IN GLASTONBURY

The goddess-in-a-box on offer in one of Glastonbury's many shops attracting goddess devotees neatly sums up the eclectic mixture of sacred and profane objects and experiences available in the small market town in the south of England. Here, we find a thriving 'spiritual economy' (Burns, 1999) where geo-physical and socio-cultural forces combine to produce mystical resources for consumers' spiritual journeys. The Goddess Conference and Festival that takes place every summer marks one such key resource, as does the Goddess Temple in the heart of the town centre. Worship of the divine feminine – the feminine counterpart challenging the patriarchal and masculine dominance of organised religions – pervades the Glastonbury atmosphere and is encoded through its landscape as well as its shopping and well-being activities.

Marion Zimmer Bradley's (1982) *The Mists of Avalon*, a historical fantasy novel narrating the legends of King Arthur from a female perspective, has played a major role in popularising Glastonbury as a centre for matriarchal religions. In her book, she documents priestess Morgaine's (Morgan le Fey) struggle to save her pagan beliefs in the face of Christian oppression. The Isle of Avalon (the ancient name for Glastonbury) is ruled by women and Bradley puts forward a utopic vision of a society that is in stark contrast to its Christian and patriarchal counterpart, Camelot. Her work very much reflects the trend popularised by second-wave feminism to develop theories of prehistoric religions based on matriarchal principles, centring around connections with nature, the body, sex and the mysteries of childbirth. Thus, Bradley uses her storyline to revalue female spirituality and paganism, as well as sexual freedom. With over one million copies printed and translations around the world (Paxton, 1999), *The Mists of Avalon* is an undoubted best-seller that has spawned much merchandising in the form of T-shirts, stickers, posters, jewellery, candles and various 'magical' blends of herbs, potions and oils.[2] It was also a popular TV miniseries on American cable channel, TNT in 2001.

Certainly, this popularisation of a matriarchal past, such as in the writings of Bradley, Starhawk and other spiritual feminists, has been widely critiqued as essentialist. Cynthia Eller is a leading voice in this respect. In her book, *The Myth of Matriarchal Prehistory: Why an Invented Past Won't Give Women a Future* (2000), she assiduously unpacks narratives of a contented goddess-worshipping pagan past, showing how it relies on unreliable and biased sources. In addition, she highlights the gender essentialism that underpins these myths, arguing that they perpetuate narrow definitions of women as those who give birth and nurture. As we previously saw in our discussions of ecofeminism, such conventional characterisations play into patriarchal hands. Other feminist scholars challenge Eller's arguments, however, as being too limited and, indeed,

Kraemer (2009) analyses seven feminist matriarchalist writings to prove this point. After showing how each defies in some way the restrictive conceptual limitations identified by Eller, she defends the genre as providing 'a much-needed corrective to patriarchy' and, hence, its inherent utopianism as a mode of critique (2009, p. 257).

In a similar vein, then, in the case study that follows, we look on Glastonbury, not as reifying essentialist notions of the divine feminine but rather as a place that fosters utopianism through its critique of the gendered nature of organised religions. To this end, we conceptualise the Glastonbury marketplace as a heterotopia, a place that facilitates the process of utopian thinking rather than its ultimate realisation. Whereas the concept of utopia envisages a future state of perfection, heterotopia is in the here and now (see Chatzidakis, Maclaran and Bradshaw [2012] for a fuller explanation). This is very much in keeping with feminist utopias that foreground experimentation and embodied practice as equally important as, if not more so than, discursive imaginings (Sargisson, 1996).

Heterotopias are marked out by their sense of contrast to dominant norms – they represent worlds within worlds, so to speak. Significantly too, the utopic dynamics they inspire are not just about thinking but also about *doing* and thus a form of utopian praxis. As shared spaces of 'otherness', heterotopias engender alternative forms of social organisation that challenge in some way our everyday norms about how space should be ordered, as do prisons, retirement homes, mental institutions, theatres and even gardens (Foucault, 1986). The thinking on heterotopias has developed over the years to focus more on the notion of difference and to conceptualise them as spaces of representation produced by alternative social relations (Hetherington, 1997; Soja, 1996). Consequently, many contemporary consumer heterotopias have come to light, such as: theme parks, shopping malls, gated communities, holiday resorts, wellness hotels, jazz clubs, and dance halls to name but a few (see Dehaene and De Cauter, 2008).

GLASTONBURY AS A MATRIARCHAL HETEROTOPIA

Here we explore Glastonbury's utopic dynamics further by elaborating it as a matriarchal heterotopia using Hetherington's (1997) three core categories of difference against which heterotopic spaces can be assessed: the built environment (or materiality), social practices, and events contained therein. Basing our analysis around these categories, we explore how Glastonbury and its surrounding landscape challenge and resist patriarchal religious culture through its thriving marketplace promoting spiritual well-being and care for the natural world.

The Materiality of Glastonbury: Shops, Landmarks and Landscape

Amid the profusion of small shops proffering colourful and creative displays of mystical merchandise stands the Goddess Temple, established in 2003 and 'devoted to bringing the Goddess alive in the world'. Here, we find a key focal point for many spiritual pilgrims, a discovery tucked away behind shops on the main high street. Being a site for meditative reflection, the temple provides an oasis of tranquillity, welcoming visitors into its darkened, incense-filled atmosphere where season-themed effigies of the goddess inspire wonderment and worship. These ingenious displays intertwine the goddess and nature to emphasise the power of their life-giving force, a message reiterated in the Goddess Temple's webpage video encouraging virtual participation in the community: 'I am the earth ... my roots stretch down into the earth and my branches reach up to the sky.'[3]

Back on the high street, shop names echo this Mother Earth goddess theme: The Speaking Tree Shop, The Goddess and the Green Man, Star Child Glastonbury, Maya of Glastonbury (Maya being the moon goddess) and Wyrdraven (the Viking shop). Alongside other outlets – The Psychic Piglet, Yin Yang and The Celtic Thread to name but a few – they present a veritable spiritual bricolage of shopping that reflects the rich mosaic of myth and legend that surrounds the region. Together with the landscape, they enable a 'pick 'n mix' approach to a personalised spirituality that challenges the strictures of traditional patriarchal religions and usually falls under the umbrella terms of New Age Spirituality or Neo-paganism (Possamai, 1999).

A major landmark is the Tor, a steep hill that dominates the landscape with a 15th-century tower rising from its summit. Generally believed to have been a site of prehistoric worship and mystical tradition on account of its strange aquifers and catacombs of caverns, the Tor is perceived by many as a portal to the other world (Mann, 2012). At the Tor's base lies the Chalice Well; thought to have been built by druids in 600 BC, its rounded contours conveying a very feminine contrast to the unmistakably phallic nature of the Tor. Because the water is reddish in colour, contemporary goddess worshippers claim this symbolises the menstrual blood of the goddess and is a materialisation of the divine feminine.

Consistent with the heterotopian notion of different social orderings existing in the same space, institutional religion also has a stake in the town, with Glastonbury Abbey located just around the corner from the main high street shops. Built on the site of the first Christian church in Britain, it dates back some 2,000 years. The Abbey too is not immune from the prevailing myths and legends, however, especially tales of Arthurian Britain that are deeply intertwined with the history of Glastonbury, such as the Isle of Avalon where King Arthur was taken to heal after his last battle. His remains and those of his wife, Queen Guinevere, were claimed to be found by medieval monks after a fire destroyed the Abbey in 1185 AD. Sceptics describe this as a timely discovery that helped to rejuvenate the Abbey's much needed pilgrimage tourism after the fire. The last section of this analysis will show how the annual goddess procession inverts the annual Christian procession that takes place from the Abbey and thereby asserts its claim to various landmarks in area.

Social Practices: Spiritual Services and Activities

It's okay not to be okay in Glastonbury and the town has a long legacy of welcoming those who feel marginal in some way from mainstream culture. Having been described as 'a place of pilgrimage for poets, mystics, weirdos and sundry unclassifiables' (Pepper, 2018) at the height of hippie culture in the 1960s, the town still retains its hippie vibe. Seen as a centre for spiritual healing, the townsfolk are very accepting of eccentricities. A vast range of spiritual services and activities comprise Glastonbury's main economy, contributing to an overriding zeitgeist that echoes ecofeminist principles of healing and oneness with(in) nature. Everywhere you look there are signs and posters for self-help, personal growth and life-coaching workshops, meditation practices, psychic readings, holistic therapies such as massage, aromatherapy, hot stones, etc., hypnotherapy and past life regression as well as many pilgrimages, retreats and festivals. The town is keenly attuned to the pagan calendar and the shops and services adapt their offerings to tie in with its ancient seasonal markers: Imbolc (1 February); Beltane (1 May); Lammas (1 August); Samhain (31 October); plus the spring and autumn equinoxes and the winter and summer solstices.

Alongside the town's emphasis on harmony and balance with the natural order is its pride in the complex layers of myth and legend that abound around Glastonbury's past as the Isle of Avalon. These facilitate matriarchal myth telling and acts of 'reclaiming' by the goddess movement that focus on *her*story (as opposed to *his*tory), embedding the goddess in the surrounding landscape to counter notions of a transcendental and monotheistic god. For example, the story of the sorceress, Morgen Le Fay, an important icon in goddess culture, has its origins in Arthurian legend as previously mentioned. Known as the 'Lady' or 'Priestess' of Avalon, she was half-human and half-fairy, recast by Marion Zimmer Bradley as a gifted woman demonised by patriarchal legend. Her eight sister Morgens represent the changing cycles of nature and are an integral part of goddess worship as well as being represented in the Goddess Temple.

Events: Pilgrimages, Pageants and Parades

For many visitors to the area, the trip to Glastonbury can be classified as a pilgrimage. The journey into the depths of rural Somerset is often challenging – there are few direct transport links and travel by car involves windy, narrow roads – and creates a sense of separation from everyday life and the sense of liminality, the otherworldliness, so essential to the spiritual aspects of the pilgrimage experience (Scott and Maclaran, 2012). There are many events acting as a draw for spiritual seekers and pagan pilgrims, whether it's Drumming the Dragon Lines (ley lines conducting Earth's male and female energies) on Glastonbury Tor;[4] climbing the Tor to watch the sunrise at the Winter or Summer Solstice;[5] or attending the Festival of Beltane with other Druids and Green Men on May Day (Ross, 2018). Of these, the aforementioned annual Goddess Conference is the biggest event, drawing 300+ participants to the town for five days of activities, talks and workshops.

The festival concludes each year with a triumphant and colourful procession that winds through the town and up to Glastonbury's mythical Tor (see Figure 5.1). The use of spectacle performs two important socio-political roles: the first as a visual pageant, the second as a moving parade (Scott and Maclaran, 2012). Led by a gigantic wicker effigy of the goddess, adorned with ribbons, feathers, beads and other charms, the goddess procession presents a vivid contrast to the more muted Christian parade that takes place earlier in the year (see Figure 5.2). The carnivalesque ambience draws many spectators to watch, admire or mock, and, as with lesbian and gay pride Mardi Gras parades (Kates, 2003), simultaneously encourages a questioning of the status quo. In a spectacular celebration of the power of the 'feminine', the goddess procession challenges the masculine dominance of public space and fights patriarchy with pageantry (Bowman, 2004). The moving nature of the parade gives the pageant additional spatial power as it makes its presence felt in key locations around the town. Claiming space in this way, it follows the same route as the Christian procession except that it makes a pointed inversion by going in the opposite direction.

Figure 5.1   The goddess parade in Glastonbury

Our vignette of Glastonbury reveals an ecofeminist heterotopia that resists patriarchal religious doctrines, even while it allows them to co-exist in the same space. This resistance is encoded through mystical materialities that engender alternative social practices and pagan pageants. Together these underpin the area's matriarchal utopics, materialised as they are in Glastonbury's goddess culture and its widespread devotion to the divine feminine. Overall these ecofeminist utopics man-

Figure 5.2   Effigy of the goddess

ifest most strongly in the quest of spiritual seekers to find oneness with the natural world, an approach that emphasises principles of holistic care (i.e. physical, emotional, social and spiritual well-being) for both oneself and the environment around us.

Yet, as our vignette also illustrates, there can be no doubt that Glastonbury is very much a consumer heterotopia with its underpinning matriarchal utopics and care-for-the-environment logics relying on market-mediated activities, events and services for their popularity. So even while Glastonbury culture promotes on the one hand ecofeminist values that challenge marketing's free use of the environment, on the other hand it also endorses a consumerist rationale that ultimately leads to further pollution and destruction of that environment. Escaping the market does indeed seem impossible except in very temporary (Kozinets,

2002) and/or local (Chatzidakis, Maclaran and Bradshaw, 2012) ways! In the next section we broaden our arguments to look at how care work more generally has been devalued in a patriarchal culture and how marketing further benefits from, and contributes to, this devaluation.

MARKETING AND CARE(LESSNESS)

The environment is not the only externality of contemporary marketing practice and consumption. Almost any marketplace exchange also imposes costs on human others, from the hidden carers that meticulously produce the various products and services that we buy (Lewis, 2016) to the so-called 'global care chains' (Hochschild, 2015) whereby immigrant workers provide paid care work to middle-class families with a view to sending money back to their own families. So-called 'care deficits' are increasingly endemic to our socio-economic system given its incapacity to prioritise people and the planet over profits (The Care Collective, 2020). These deficits are reflective of a deep-seated contradiction: our socio-economic system's reliance on human and non-human forms of life on the one hand, and their parallel destruction as part of its ongoing quest for capital accumulation (Fraser, 2016a, 2016b). Capitalist markets offer 'care fixes' such as the outsourcing of care to cheaper migrant workers, or the commodification and automation of care by using information and assistive technologies (Dowling, 2020). At best, such fixes push further down the road some of the manifestations of our current care crisis, but they cannot address its structural causes.

Over the last ten years, however, and even more so after the advent of the coronavirus pandemic, care is increasingly recognised as a latent, often invisible activity that has remained, for various historical and political reasons, heavily gendered and racialised. Within feminist theory, this is directly linked with its emphasis on social reproduction rather than production, that is all the labour needed to maintain and reproduce human lives. Socially reproductive labour is not accounted for in the mainstream market system, yet it is essential for its survival, and current socio-economic systems would literally collapse if this status quo was about to change. 'Wages for housework' (Federici, 1975), for instance, is a historic feminist movement that attempted to make this very point, when women demanded that the unpaid care work that takes place in the home is (financially) recognised. In the UK alone, it is estimated that the hidden cost of household work such as doing the laundry and looking after one's children is worth well over a £1 trillion per year – more than the value of the country's retail and manufacturing output combined (Rawlinson, 2018).

How is marketing and consumption implicated in this? First by fore-grounding, glamourising and normalising forms of market-mediated care at the expense of alternative, potentially superior forms of care provision such as those provided by families, communities and states. A broader assumption within the alternative and feminist economics literature is that care that is provided by markets is often incompatible with key care values such as attentive listening, empathy, devotion, and so on (e.g. The Care Collective 2020). However, marketing is by design invested in promoting market as opposed to non-market mediated forms of care provision. Its archetypal subject remains the consumer, as opposed to say the parent, student, patient or citizen. This has profound implications in terms of which ideologies, logics and practices of care giving and receiving are normalised and which ones are seen as rather unconventional, inferior or less desired. Second, marketing obscures the systemic carelessness of much business activity through campaigns that present corporations as always caring and a positive force of society. The latter is encapsulated not only in the various forms of greenwashing and wokewashing discussed in earlier chapters, but also the advent of a more recent variant, carewashing.

MARKETING AND THE OUTSOURCING OF EVERYTHING

The privatised care sector represents one of the world's most thriving industries, promising to address an ever-more expansive set of care needs via the marketplace. For example, in www.care.com, individuals can find rated carers for anything they want, from childcare to house-keeping and special needs. Meanwhile, once radical notions of self-care and wellness now represent washed down, multi-billion and extremely lucrative economic sectors (Mahdawi, 2020). Such sectors reframe care as a highly individualised choice that is best served through a series of marketplace solutions and 'treats' (Dowling, 2020). Entirely absent and, indeed, disavowed, is any idea that care is a collective responsibility and that it is more meaningfully given and received, under conditions that allow the flourishing of *all* human and non-human forms of life (The Care Collective, 2020).

However the marketing and marketisation of care affects a myriad of other, rather more banal consumption contexts, from buying takeaway food as opposed to preparing it to paying babysitters and domestic cleaners. It is fair to say that an increasing number of caring activities that were traditionally performed by families, communities and states are now increasingly outsourced and packaged for sale in the marketplace: from buying ready-made food as opposed to preparing and eating food together to paying for services that were once (and still are, in some countries) provided by welfare states, such as health, education and housing. But why is this a problem? Various consumer studies (as well as a broader chorus of interdisciplinary literature) have shown the difficulties and contradictions entailed in marketising care (e.g. Parsons et al., 2021; Chatzidakis, 2022). For instance, although buying ready-made food can be a practical solution to the challenges of hectic family lives, if overdone it can expose the missed value of homemade food as a sign of true parental devotion and care (Moisio, Arnould and Price, 2004). Consumer research has shown that the amount of effort someone puts into various caring activities is paramount to the perceived symbolic meaning and quality of care (Garcia-Rada et al., 2021). It seems that, as noted above, many non-market attributes of care, such as empathy, devotion and attentive listening, cannot be marketised without losing their value.

Beyond specific qualities of care, however, and the extent to which they can be marketised without being undermined, another key – and rather more significant – problem is that markets also reproduce specific 'ideologies of care' (Dowling, 2020) at the expense of others. For instance, when we approach higher education or healthcare as customers rather than students or patients, we end up placing a whole different set of demands on our teachers and doctors, who are viewed instead as service providers. Below we illustrate how market-infused ideologies of care have begun interpenetrating traditional non-market realms of care provision such as households, communities and states (building on Chatzidakis, 2022).

Households: Thanks to the seminal work of anthropologists such as Danny Miller (2012), everyday consumption is now acknowledged as a realm that hardly ever reflects an outright selfish and individualist ethos. In fact, it is more commonly done with others in mind, and indeed primarily significant others, i.e. family members (e.g. Cappellini, Marshall and Parsons, 2016). Accordingly, consumer scholars have acknowledged the central role of markets and consumption in care provision and associated benefits such as maintaining a sense of familial care and identity, and even markets' role in advancing women's emancipation (Scott, 2006).

However the (Western-centric) model of market-mediated familial care reproduces rather specific ideologies of caring and ideas of (worthy) selfhood. For instance, according to Lareau (2000), the underlying logic of middle-class familial consumption is that of 'concerted cultivation'; in other words, parents spend as much money as they can to enhance their children's social, cultural and economic capital. Akin to notions of intensive helicopter or snowplough parenting, middle-class and upwardly mobile families constantly strive to outcompete each other (the well-known model of 'catching up with the Joneses'), by intensively parenting their children and making sure they make the right choices in life. Put differently, the underlying ideology of care relies on consumerism and competitive individualism. It is an ideology that leaves little space or time to care for less resourced families or others that are beyond 'people like us'. Thus, middle-class consumerist families may also be complicit in the reproduction of intersectional injustices through 'care chains' (Hochschild, 2015); that is, the outsourcing of household labour to migrant women who in turn send their earnings back to their own families. Of course, they are also oblivious to the hidden histories and social relations underlying the production chains of all commodities that enter the field of domestic caregiving. As Holly Lewis (2016, p. 10) puts it in *The Politics of Everybody*:

> Each of us … has a network of invisible caretakers scattered across the globe, fulfilling tasks once performed within the community. People we don't know stitch together our underwear, mine the metals used to make the machines that make our bicycles and pots, harvest our grain, grind the sand to make our drinking glasses. Sometimes our invisible caretakers live in town: lifting boxes from pallets, grading our term papers, preparing food in the backs of restaurants, cleaning our shit off public toilets.

Communities: Another key pillar of care provision is communities, comprising not just the care we receive from our neighbours and our community groups but also local organsations (e.g. NGOs, social enterprises) and religious groups. A consistent trend across various countries, however, has been that such community relations are market mediated. Brand communities (Muniz and O'Guinn, 2001), subcultures of consumption (Schouten and McAlexander, 1995) or consumer 'tribes' (Cova, Kozinets and Shankar, 2007) are increasingly replacing more traditional forms of sociality and rely on social ties that are formed through shared interests in brands, products, leisure activities and consumption practices. On the one hand, some have suggested that such opportunities offered by markets and commercialisation are not necessarily unwelcome (e.g. Streeck, 2012). They represent new types of what Simmel called *Vergesellschaftung* or 'sociation' – that is, ways in which individuals link up with others and thereby help define their identity and place in the world.

On the other hand, various scholars have emphasised that the opportunities offered by market-mediated communities in terms of care provision are in some fundamental ways inadequate. According to Steve Miles (2010), for instance, they are by and large based on the notion of 'complicit' (rather than genuine) communality (and indeed care). Commoditised spaces cannot be communal or caring enough because they are designed to maximise opportunities for profit making and they exclude those that do not have the means to participate in them. Concurrently, through offering a sense of a bygone community ethos, they end up being antagonistic to the more radical social and community infrastructures that are urgently needed for the provision of universal community care: from community libraries and libraries of things to shared urban spaces, parks, local arts centres, and more transparent and democratic forms of local governance (e.g. radical municipalism; The Care Collective, 2020).

Another problem with marketised or market-mediated communities is that they are organised, by definition, around common (consumer) identities and interests. They therefore build upon ideologies of possessive individualism: consumers participate in them as individuals who simply exert greater value by being part of them as opposed to members of communities who put their collective interest over and above individual ones (Gilbert, 2013). They leave no space for more radical ways of caring for one another and for extending care across difference and distance.

States: The infusion of market logics is even more pronounced in the realm of state-based care provision. Here, ideologies of marketised and commoditised care have reached unprecedented scale. Realms of collective care and welfare, once traditionally viewed as civic are increasingly privatised, including healthcare, education, childcare, elderly care and housing. The consequences for the amount and type of support we receive from the state are far-reaching. First, many scholars have pointed out that the marketisation of public services and infrastructures often results in deteriorating their quality whilst also making them more expensive and undermining their long-term sustainability (Bondurant, 2013;

Horton, 2019). Concurrently, individuals are ideologically transformed from citizens to consumers, and from care seekers into 'care customers' (e.g. Farris and Marchetti, 2017). This inevitably redefines the way they understand their surrounding world. The marketisation of traditional non-market realms comes with the adoption of a specific vocabulary, one that includes words such as customer and consumer rather than citizen, choice and markets rather than community ties, self-interest rather than solidarity, and individual rather than collective (Massey, 2013). These words do not simply describe reality; they are performative of it. They inform our everyday dreams and fantasies, producing and reproducing our subjectivities (ibid.). Focusing on a services marketing context, Parsons et al. (2021) observe how a marketised care orientation reproduces highly individualised and hierarchical logics that are incompatible with the cultivation of more meaningful relationships and a collective sense of shared responsibility.

More profoundly, then, the marketisation of public goods and collective care infrastructures 'corrupts' the care values cherished in our societies. According to Michael Sandel (2012), the world-renowned Harvard-based philosopher, market values crowd out non-market values. A typical example is attempts to monetise blood giving and which, rather counterintuitively, commonly result in fewer donations. Sandel's explanation is that once a caring practice such as blood donating is reframed as an instrumentalised choice, individuals no longer feel the responsibility to care for others. Similarly, in the context of healthcare, Mol (2008) explains how the 'logic of (customer) choice' is radically opposed to the 'logic of care'. Care values such as attentiveness, adaptability, empathetic listening, devotion cannot be accounted by market metrics. Therefore sociologists such as Beverley Skeggs (2014) emphasise that 'caring that is offered as a gift beyond exchange relations is of a different form to the relations established to promote and reproduce the logic of capital. Caring offers us a different way of being in the world, relating to others as if they matter, with attentiveness and compassion, beyond exchange' (p. 13). A more genuinely caring orientation would therefore encourage a deeper appreciation of our common fate and interdependence, one that would insist on embracing (and demarketising) our commons while working collectively towards their repair and maintenance.

CAREWASHING

Beyond the role of markets and consumerism in foregrounding and normalising specific ideologies of care at the expense of others, marketing also plays a more specific part in reframing and legitimising the activities of uncaring corporations. 'Carewashing' refers to communication strategies designed to demonstrate how 'caring' a corporation is in ways that commonly obscure that corporation's actual destructive social and environmental impacts (The Care Collective, 2020). It can be viewed as the latest iteration of explicit corporate gestures in support of social and environmental causes which are driven by both reputational and broader legitimacy concerns around the role of corporations in society. Although part of a longer genealogy of the corporate wash-list – from whitewashing to greenwashing to wokewashing and femmewashing – carewashing also has particularities, not least because it is directly addressing the importance of care and care work, as well as the potential role of corporations in a (more) caring world amidst a variety of looming crises. Below we draw from Chatzidakis and Littler (2022) to illustrate some characteristic examples that point to both the extensiveness of carewashing and some of its different manifestations.

First, carewashing often involves rebranding a particular service or product as essential to the facilitation of our care needs. For example, a 2020 Instagram advert of the soap Carex used the hashtag '#whywecarex', to tell us that 'every squirt and splodge keeps those hands safe and protected'. Likewise, an advert by Dove reminded us that washing our hands is one of the best ways to take care of our loved ones during the coronavirus pandemic. Such adverts capitalised on the prioritisation of handwashing as a means of preventing the pandemic before the primarily airborne nature of the virus became widespread knowledge. Meanwhile, these brands did little to prevent the excessive and unfair pricing of sanitising and cleaning products and have continued to see huge profits from surging sales up to the present day. In addition, they also continue to be owned by large multi-nationals that have highly questionable social and environmental impacts. Carex, for instance is owned by PZ Cussons, a company that scores 8/20 on its ethical record in the Ethical Consumer Index and which has been explicitly targeted by Greenpeace over its environmental record, particularly its use of palm oil.[6] Dove is owned by Unilever, a company renowned for its ethical and 'purposive' branding and which however continues to be in the spotlight for various less-positive activities. For instance, in 2019 the corporation was charged with being in the global top 10 of plastic polluters (Segran, 2019) and has come under fire for anti-union violence in South Africa (it is 'a British company' but most workers are overseas).[7] This is exactly what is meant by the contradictory (if not hypocritical) nature of carewashing.

Carewashing also commonly builds on the idea that brands can be used as a resource and/or facilitator of community care. The telecommunications company giffgaff, for example, drew on tropes of community mutual aid, care and solidarity by attesting, in one of its 2020 campaigns, that 'a good community would be made up of caring individuals'. Similarly, for detergent brand Fairy, 'community is kindness'. Other brands, such as HSBC emphasised the role of community 'heroes'. The company expressed on Instagram how grateful it was/we were to 'all our local heroes', from 'farmers to pharmacists' for 'going above and beyond'. It pronounced that we are all 'part of something far, far bigger'. Similarly, Uber thanked 'all drivers, for moving what matters', including nurses and paramedics. Such adverts can be readily understood as practices of 'meaning transfer' (McCracken, 1986), whereby meanings generated within the wider realm of culture and society are appropriated and transferred into the consumption experience of specific brands.

In other instances, carewashing reflects more outright opportunistic attempts to counteract bad publicity and to aggressively represent the corporation under a more positive light. Amazon, for instance, a corporation accused of repeatedly failing to care for its workers' health and safety standards during the coronavirus pandemic – to the extent that it was ordered by court to close its French factories (Hern, 2020) – still went ahead with a campaign claiming the exact opposite: 'Keeping our people safe while getting you the things you need has never been more important.' Altogether then, carewashing can be viewed as part of a longer genealogy of corporate attempts to represent themselves as socially responsible or caring, and in doing so legitimise their role and place in society. Although it is certainly true that some corporations can be understood as more 'caring' than others, it is also the case that on the whole, the idea that is normalised across the various marketing communications is that the corporate sector 'cares'. There is conspicuously less emphasis on corporations' negative social and environmental impacts or that, after all, most corporations are by design required to care for profits before people and the planet. In this sense and regardless of the exact extent to which corporate carelessness is endemic, marketing is responsible for normalising and (over)idealising the corporation as a caring institution and an indisputably positive force for society.

NOTES

1. The 'notion of pure, unchanging, and often biologically based qualities' (Norgaard, 1998, p. 492).
2. See, for example, https://www.etsy.com/market/mists_of_avalon
3. Watch the virtual Goddess Temple video at: https://goddesstemple.co.uk/
4. See a presentation of our engagement in this workshop at https://www.slideshare.net/alwayspbraun/drumming-the-dragon-lines
5. Get the feel for this ritual: https://www.youtube.com/watch?v=4-qoLnxYau0
6. It also scores 8/20 on the Ethical Consumer Index: https://www.ethicalconsumer.org/health-beauty/shopping-guide/ethical-soap and https://www.campaignlive.co.uk/article/carex-maker-hits-back-greenpeace-sustainability-spat/1459928
7. https://www.ethicalconsumer.org/company-profile/unilever

6. Who cares for the marketing organisation?

The organisational aspects of marketing are also gendered. Women in marketing are most likely to be in some type of customer facing role, whereas their male colleagues are likely to be found in more strategic marketing roles that are often higher ranking, better paid and more likely to be at board level (Maclaran, Catterall and Stevens, 1997). Women are stereotypically seen as being appropriate for the caring aspects of the organisation. In many ways, little seems to have changed over the last 20 years. Although there are many more women than men in marketing associate positions (two-thirds female to one-third male),[1] there continues to be many more men in senior positions (one-third female to two-thirds male) in the United Kingdom despite more encouraging trends in the US.[2] Whereas the previous chapter focused on certain marketing externalities, now we move to marketing's internalities as we look more closely at who does what marketing work and the gendered nature of specific roles and areas within our profession. First, however, to set the gendered workplace scene, we broaden our view to consider issues around the division of labour more generally. Then we highlight the feminisation of both the marketing workplace and the marketing discourse, before considering how feminist ethics may apply in the context of marketing's organisational and professional values.

GENDERED DIVISIONS OF LABOUR

The gendered division of labour is, of course, broader to the evolution of our current socio-economic system and the deeply entrenched subordination of feminised, social reproductive labour (aka the 'making of people') to masculine productive (aka the 'making of profit') labour (e.g. Arruzza, Bhattacharya and Fraser, 2019). It is no secret, however, that particular professions – as well as roles and functions within them – are also perceived as men's or women's worlds (Calas and Smircich, 1991). Despite major, or at least more explicit, drives towards gender equality in organisational life, occupational segregation is still alive and well, as Ibáñez and García-Mingo (2021) vividly depict in their research of seven traditionally male occupations that reveals how mechanisms of social closure operate to ensure the continued exclusion of women. These occupations delimit themselves by constructing gendered identities and communities operating at structural, professional and organisational levels. Granted this research focuses on areas that have long-standing associations with masculinity (police, construction, train drivers, etc.), but business occupations are also often segregated, albeit in more subtle ways, especially with regard to professional status. In the accountancy profession a division developed between high-powered consultancy specialisms and the more mundane auditing roles, with many more women in the latter or in smaller companies where remuneration is less (Ciancanelli et al., 1990; Broadbent and Kirkham, 2008). Similarly, women in public relations are more likely to be allocated the technical-type roles (coordinating events and appeasing customers) while men have the more prestigious, higher-earning positions (Krider and Ross, 1997), a glass ceiling that still exists for many women in PR today (Liedermann, 2020). Gender segregation in the public administrative sector is often to the detriment of public policy outcomes as demonstrated in a recent study by Krøtel, Ashworth and Villadsen (2019). And, despite a high prevalence of client-facing roles plus a reliance on stereotypically feminine skills such as intuition and social interaction, advertising too is an industry where women are rarely seen in leadership positions. In fact, the creative side of advertising is well-documented to be male dominated even though women make up 50 per cent of the advertising industry's workforce (Thompson-Whiteside, 2020). Depressingly, little seems to have changed since Alvesson's study (1998) of a Swedish advertising agency (discussed more fully in Chapter 1) showing how this feminised context triggered the structuring of gender relations within the agency to restore feelings of masculinity.

Such studies are evidence that, even though there is increasing feminisation of the workplace more generally, change to existing power structures remains slow with less readily detectable horizontal gender segregation still flourishing. As a result, even after a profession has been feminised, women continue to be excluded from strategic decision-making roles or, if included, may be forced to adapt to a masculine culture to get ahead or at best the principles of 'neoliberal' or 'boardroom feminism' (Rottenberg, 2018). Such liberal versions of feminism celebrate the placement of more women in positions of power but fall short in scrutinising whether these women continue the harmful and oppressive practices of their male predecessors. This is why more radical and genuinely egalitarian versions of feminism insist on (gender) justice and accountability at *all* levels of the organisation (e.g. Arruzza et al., 2019). Notwithstanding, another significant factor is the feminisation of a specific role or discipline and its concomitant drop in status. Consider, for example, research on the banking sector in Western Europe that revealed how the feminisation of local branch management coincided with organisational restructuring that downgraded the decision-making authority and scope of branch management (Tienari, Quack and Theobald, 1999). As its status eroded, skills required for branch management became those traditionally associated with females and in terms of upward career mobility in the banking structure, it became a dead end (Maclaran and Catterall, 2000).

Another good example is personnel management, originally seen as a welfare role within organisations; a profession that became attractive to women due to male labour shortages as businesses began to expand this function in the 1970s (Roos and Manley, 1996). With women perceived as stereotypically more suited to the role, the profession quickly feminised. As it did so, however, men lost interest in being personnel managers and feminisation resulted in lower earnings as well as loss of professional status. Significantly, the profession made a deliberate attempt to regain its status by repositioning itself as Human Resource Management (rather than welfare) and aligning its focus with more strategic aspects such as downsizing and so forth (Legge, 1987). Yet, although there is now a much higher proportion of women in managerial positions within HRM today, it is still seen as stereotypically female and a way for many corporations to include token representation of women at board level (Faugoo, 2011).

THE FEMINISATION OF MARKETING

When it comes to the feminisation of marketing, there are two aspects to consider: (1) the feminisation of the marketing workforce; and (2) the feminisation of the marketing discourse (Maclaran and Catterall, 2000). First, in relation to the former, the last two decades have seen increasing proportions of females to males studying marketing and entering the marketing profession. Women dominate in customer-facing roles such as marketing research, public relations and customer service/care. Nevertheless, there have been few studies on women who work in the profession. A long-standing exception is a study on women marketing managers that revealed female informants felt excluded from strategic decision-making and resented being given the less valued support roles (Maclaran, Catterall and Stevens, 1997). The findings of this research highlighted a 'glasshouse effect' where women felt boxed in all sides, with horizontal as well as vertical barriers to the progression of their marketing careers. Above all, informants confirmed what Gherardi (1995, p. 11) describes as 'the great male saga of conquest (of new markets) and of campaigns (to launch new products)'. In contrast, the service side of marketing 'echoes to the language of care, of concern for needs and of relationality' (p. 12). As one female marketing manager commented about the prevailing attitude in her firm, 'girls are all right for the advertising jobs, etc., but when it gets to the commercial stuff, that's for the boys'. Others agreed, indicating they were expected to perform the 'decorative', 'cosmetic' and 'smiling' roles, such as customer service and PR.

Certainly, this picture has been changing over the last 20 years with more females in director-level marketing positions and 52 per cent of CMOs (Chief Marketing Officers) in North America are now women (Burt, 2021), although the UK lags considerably behind in this respect[3]. However, such statistics do not consider the caveats of neoliberal and boardroom feminism (noted above). In addition, racial diversity is highly problematic, with only 13 per cent of CMOs in North America coming from racially diverse backgrounds (Burt, 2021), so it seems there is still a long way to go in the pursuit of a truly diverse and egalitarian marketing workforce. Moreover, more research is needed into the working lives of female CMOs to understand more about their roles and whether, like female HRM directors, the marketing role is perceived as an appropriate way to have more women at board level. This is particularly likely given that only 5 per cent of Fortune 500 companies have women CEOs and women hold only 10 per cent of leadership positions in S&P 1500 companies[4] (Getchell and Beitelspacher, 2020).

The Forbes World's Most Influential CMOs list included 31 women out of 50 chief marketing officers in 2019. Even with this potentially encouraging sign, the Forbes data also revealed that media give more attention to male CMOs, with men accumulating 1,959 news mentions in contrast to female CMOs' total of 1,050 mentions. In their study of the discourse around female CMOs, Getchell and Beitelspacher (2020) examined this more closely, identifying how media referred to the women on the Forbes list with more stereotypically feminine descriptors and applied fewer words with leadership associations. Male CMOs, on the other hand, were more likely to be portrayed as 'strong', industry-shaping', 'fearless' and 'confident'. Even when words such as 'powerful' were used in the descriptors for females, it tended to be in conjunction with the female CMOs' support for other women.

Gender ideology at work in this way can impact on women's career progression, making them feel obliged to follow traditional gender stereotypes or, indeed, to do the reverse, and buy into a masculine culture in order to progress their careers. Again, media can play a crucial role in perpetuating such normative gender assumptions. This proved to be the case in relation to the social enterprise of Sheena Matheiken, a disaffected advertising executive who successfully promoted socially conscious consumption through The Uniform Project, so named because her challenge was to wear the same little black dress every day for a year. Her project raised over $US100,000 for charity as she transformed her 'uniform' in creative ways each day and communicated these to an expanding group of followers. Despite Matheiken's efforts to build a collective impetus around her venture, what began as a polyvocal enterprise to make the voices of beneficiaries in rural India heard, mutated into a singular heroic quest when mediated in the popular press. This framing of her creative marketing strategy reflected gendered business tropes around entrepreneurship more broadly (Kravets, Preece and Maclaran, 2020).

The second aspect for consideration here is the feminisation of the marketing discourse, particularly in relation to relationship marketing and mass customisation. With regard to the latter, Fischer (2000) shows that in contrast to mass marketing which involves 'bombarding', 'pushing' and 'soliciting', 'mass customisation is a much kinder and gentler creature: it is "responsive", it "collaborates", it "conducts a dialogue"'. So, whereas the discourse of mass marketing employs terms that are culturally associated with maleness, mass customisation, on the other hand, embodies traits associated with femaleness. However, this apparently more feminised discourse contains themes of stalking, kidnapping and capturing customers. Fischer comments that 'a captive customer who is satisfied in an ever-greater number of ways is *still* a captive: the point of keeping the target satisfied is to continue to control them. And this control is intended to be permanent.' This reinforces Hopton's (1999) point that the rise of managerialism, in spite of its feminine rhetoric of cooperative working, team building and flattened hierarchies, merely replaces militarism in maintaining the power base of a patriarchal state and that team development initiatives can be construed as a type of hypermasculinity.

Similar themes have been identified in relationship marketing discourses and practices that heralded an emphasis on emotional and social skills – stereotypically perceived as softer, feminine skills – to replace more task-oriented, 'masculine' work (Tynan, 1997). The relationship-building emphasis notwithstanding, Fournier, Dobscha and Mick (1998) suggest: 'When people talk of their lives as consumers they do not praise their so-called corporate partners. Rather, the consumer feels isolated in a threatening marketplace where confusion, stress and manipulation are all commonplace.' Nor is it appropriate to conceive of relationship marketing as based on a 'happy marriage' metaphor because this overlooks the potential dysfunctionality of the relationship (Tynan, 1997; O'Malley and Tynan, 1999). Furthermore, unlike marriage, the relationship between the parties is an unequal one, with the company usually having more power than the consumer. This is increasingly true with contemporary data mining techniques quickly identifying non-profitable customers to shed them or, at least, alter customer service levels to reflect their business value.

Even given its more overtly caring rhetoric, it remains difficult to ignore the military language underpinning much of marketing's strategic discourse with its emphasis on the 'cut and thrust values' of targeting and penetration (Desmond, 1997; Stevens, 2018). Terms like 'launching a campaign', 'capturing' marketing share, 'strategic positioning' and 'outflanking' the competition all have military roots (Lutkins, 2017). Militarism still percolates the more feminised discourse of customer service with the notion of 'frontline' staff where, of course, more women are likely to be in the direct line of fire (Stevens, 2018). And, in keeping with what we know about feminisation causing status insecurity, we now seem to be seeing a resurgence of what are traditionally considered masculine values. Take, for example, the increasing domination of customer relationship management by big data analytics with its renewed emphasis on the militaristic notion of 'tracking' consumers through surveillance logics based on scientific algorithms. Recalling what Deem (2003) described as the emergence of a 'macho-masculinity' in management theory and practice, in turn these militaristic logics challenge and trivialise the softer, service side of customer management with its emphasis on care and emotional labour (Dasu and Chase, 2010).

.

IN THE FRONTLINE FIRING LINE: AESTHETIC AND EMOTIONAL LABOUR

Frontline staff are generally expected to enact an organisation's customer service strategy, with its concomitant requirements for them to remain flexible and adaptable to customer demands, and to remain cheerful and friendly, or even humble, if required by the situation (Lovelock, Wirtz and Chew, 2009). Interpersonal skills such as empathy and listening are valued above all else, with a long list of other emotional responses expected to be on tap at any given moment in a service interaction: helpfulness, communicative abilities, courtesy, friendliness, knowledge and reliability to name but a few. All these requirements invoke a subject position that is coded feminine on account of women's long-standing cultural associations with matters relational and emotional. At this point it is useful to recall Arlie Hochschild's (1983) seminal work on *The Managed Heart*, a study of Delta Airlines female flight attendants and bill collectors (male and female). Here she first introduced the notion of 'emotional labour', a term used to convey how service staff create exchange value through managing their feelings to maintain a positive persona even in the event of negative customer interactions. And, emotional labour does not just manage inner feelings, it is just as much about managing bodily reactions, as Knights and Thanem (2005) have argued in their critique of the disembodied aspects of Hochschild's work and, in particular, her distinction between physical and emotional labour. They highlight the importance of various facial and body movements, as well as voice intonations that are direct corporeal effects of emotional labour and are a crucial part of much routinised service work.

Shifting the emphasis more clearly to management of the body in service work, studies on aesthetic labour further challenge the corporeal oversight that prevails in the emotional labour literature (e.g. Witz, Warhurst and Nickson, 2003) although they tend to do this at the expense of the inner emotional labour required (Knights and Thanem, 2005). The body of scholarship on aesthetic labour foregrounds how the corporeality of employees is frequently appropriated, controlled and, indeed, commodified in order to enhance the customer experience in many industries. Concepts like employee branding emphasise the requirement for employees to have the 'right look' for the organisation, a requirement that implies that an employee's appearance and demeanour are all part of the overall brand identity. If successful as a strategy, employees internalise the brand image to become brand ambassadors, projecting their employer's brand identity in their everyday activities and interactions. Corporations such as Google famously create innovative workplace environments and supply free meals and leisure facilities for staff to encourage this type of brand internalisation.

Often, too, aesthetic labour becomes sexualised labour when innuendo is used, especially through advertising and other marketing communications techniques that include suggestive remarks around company personnel to encourage the customer to interpret the brand aesthetic in sexualised ways (Spiess and Waring, 2005). Most often, although not always, sexualised labour concerns female staff. We see this very clearly in the case of Virgin Airlines' 'Still Red Hot' campaign in 2009 that, even as it offers a parody of airline iconography in the 1980s, encourages a postfeminist reading of agentic female sexuality that ignores the discrimination perpetuated by the industry (Duffy, Hancock and Tyler, 2017). Apart from air travel, the hospitality sector is another area that frequently utilises more sexualised service interactions to beguile the customer. The American chain of restaurants, Hooters, unashamedly continues to sell sexualised labour as a crucial part of its service delivery – its infamous name being a slang term in the US for a woman's breasts. The female staff sport uniforms of skimpy orange shorts combined with low-cut tops that overtly sexualise them. Hooters' current website advertises a career as a Hooters Girl as being 'an honor bestowed upon only the most entertaining, goal oriented, glamorous and charismatic women. Hooters Girls have that special gift for making every guest feel welcome.' And, as if we've rolled back feminism 50 years: 'She'll have all kinds of opportunities – like appearing in the annual Hooters Swimsuit Calendar.'

Of course, sexualised labour is not confined to women alone and Abercrombie and Fitch as well as its sister brand, Hollister, gained notoriety for using male and female retail workers as models in store to represent the brand. Shirtless male models who flaunted their perfect abs gave the brands their high profile and athletic positioning among a target youth market for many years. Much controversy ensued and the discriminatory practices around Abercrombie and Fitch's emphasis on white beauty and athletic bodies have been well documented (Walters, 2016). The brands have now abandoned the half-clad look and changed their nightclub aesthetics to better reflect the interests of a more woke youth generation (Hanbury, 2018).

There can be no doubt, nonetheless, that service work continues to be dominated by female staff who are stereotypically perceived as being more suitable to pleasing the customer. Its feminisation is not just problematic as regards the commodification of affect in the ways we have discussed above. A significant issue is the alienation of certain groups of men from service work because of its feminine associations, an alienation that ensures feminisation becomes self-perpetuating. The growth of the service economy over the last 30 years has marked the decline of industrial-type manual work, traditionally undertaken by low-skilled male workers. Still, many unemployed young men are unwilling to take jobs that might be available in the service sector on account of three key threats to their masculinity (Lupton, 2000): (1) the risk of being feminised themselves; (2) lack of homosocial relations to reinforce their masculinity; and (3) fear of being perceived as effeminate by their peers. Indeed, the deference required to serve a customer plus high levels of emotion management are completely opposed to the rugged masculinity of working-class men (McDowell, 2003), especially given that hard manual work is a crucial component of this classed identity (Skeggs, 1997). Research further shows that unemployed men from working-class backgrounds may lack confidence in seeking out interactive service roles because of the perceived patience required as well as the management of their emotions (Nixon, 2009). Significantly, too, the classed nature of many servicescapes is enacted through employees' complete self-subordination to clients in order to enhance the latter's status in the social hierarchy (Dion and Borraz, 2017), a complete anathema to many working-class men whose sense of self includes the valorisation of not being middle class (Skeggs, 1997).

Much feminist scholarship on embodiment – as discussed already in Chapter 1 – deconstructs the traditional Cartesian mind/body split to better synthesise corporeal and emotional elements, as for example in the notion of 'feeling bodies' (Stevens, 2018). This work emphasises both the affective powers of bodies and the somatic manifestations of emotions (Knights and Thanem, 2005). In other words, the feelings we experience through bodily sensations directly affect our emotions, whether spontaneous or managed. Importantly, too, social context influences our displays of emotions and control of our bodies, regulating what is acceptable or not, with different types of display deemed appropriate for men or women. The 'politics of appearance' (Elias, Gill and Scharff, 2017) are, therefore, a long-standing focus of feminist scholarship with debates shifting more recently to intersectional and transnational critiques of beauty ideals and the notion of feminine capital that underpins them. For example, whereas being white (or 'whiter'), youthful and good-looking increases someone's perceived value or capital, being darker skinned, ageing and blemished all militate against accruing value (Jha, 2016). If we add to this the current digital surveillance of women's bodies, not only through the digital media gaze, but also through many self-monitoring/-tracking devices, we arrive at a type of aesthetic labour inspired by neoliberalism whereby beauty resources play a crucial role in an entrepreneurial subjectivity:

> In the hypervisible landscape of popular culture the body is recognised as the object of women's labour: it is her asset, her product, her brand and her gateway to freedom and empowerment in a neoliberal market economy. (Winch, 2015, p. 233)

Such a neoliberal beauty culture runs deep in women's psyches, responsibilising the need to look good (Elias et al., 2017). In other words, if we feel fat or ugly, it's up to us to fix ourselves. The implications of this neoliberal message are clear: the problem is devolved to an individual and personalised level rather than being seen as stemming from macro-level cultural (patriarchal) effects that present a collective challenge for women. In turn, the intensification of beauty culture to which Elias et al. (2017) refer feeds what they term 'aesthetic entrepreneurship' (p. 37). Nowhere is this type of entrepreneurship more prevalent than in the domain of influencer marketing where feminine capital is frequently employed in very sexualised ways, an aesthetic described by Drenten, Gurrieri and Tyler (2020) as 'porn chic' in their study of 172 female influencers on Instagram. Closely related to the wider pornification of culture (Dines, 2010), overt self-sexualisation claims more attention and, hence, more monetary opportunities. Yet, although adding value, such sexual objectification also brought many more instances of online sexual harassment and bullying.

CAN THE (MARKETING) ORGANISATION CARE?

So far we have discussed the gendering of (marketing) labour and discourse. Yet, when it comes to marketing's internalities, another significant set of questions arise in relation to the nature of the marketing organisation. Are organisations themselves gendered? What would a more feminist organisation look like?

To respond to such questions, we return to the notion of care. Here, however, we are more interested in a feminist understanding of care as an overall 'ethic' or 'orientation'. Culturally, care is in stark contrast with the typically masculine competitive and market-driven cultures that exist within most organisations, as it comprises qualities such as empathy, attentive listening and compassion. All of these are socially coded as feminine and are often invisibilised, undervalued or simply seen as irrelevant within organisations. Yet, as we argue below, the revaluing and foregrounding of care is essential if gender equality is to be taken seriously at the organisational level (and beyond).

Care ethics represents a now established empirical and philosophical line of enquiry that is commonly associated with women and feminism. Perhaps its most essential feature is the emphasis on relationality, as opposed to impartiality, which is often the basis for contrasting care ethics with justice ethics. For example, many organisations are increasingly evaluated on the basis of how 'just' they are. A plethora of certifications – from the Athena Swan for UK universities to the 'EDGE' and 'Fair Pay' certifications used in the business world – aim to showcase the steps organisations have taken to redress gender-based pay gaps. Furthermore, with the advent of stakeholder theory, questions of justice have extended not only to those who work within specific organisations, but to a variety of other stakeholders who are affected by their operations, such as investors, users and customers, local communities, society and the environment at large. Care ethics scholars would argue that such questions of justice are not enough: one needs to pay closer attention to the webs of interpersonal relations *within* the organisation, and the context-bound responses to the care needs of others.

One of the most influential works on care ethics is Carol Gilligan's *In a Different Voice* (1982). In this, Gilligan outlines her psychological exploration of women's moral reasoning, beginning with the assumption that psychologists and moral philosophers more generally, for far too long, had 'assumed a culture in which men were the measure of humanity, and autonomy and rationality ("masculine" qualities) were the markers of maturity. It was a culture that counted on women not speaking for themselves' (Gilligan, 2011, pp. 16–17). Drawing on her studies, Gilligan outlines a feminine perspective to ethical reasoning. Among others, she takes on Kohlberg's famous psychological stages of moral development to illustrate its blindness to a distinct mode of thinking and doing that is commonly found in women; a mode that foregrounds emotions and human relationships rather than rationality, interdependence rather than impartiality, and more generally a deeper, more embedded perspective of care needs and their satisfaction. Previously, Kohlberg and his followers had assumed that girls and women did not develop their moral abilities to what they identified as 'the highest levels' of morality, those associated with abstract and impartial reasoning. Gilligan's ground-breaking contribution exposed their androcentric bias and foregrounded feminine ethics of care as an equally legitimate mode of reasoning that is distinct from the ethics of justice.

Alongside Carol Gilligan, other famous female philosophers and scholars, such as Nel Noddings, Joan Tronto, Eva Kittay, Nancy Chodorow and Virginia Held, helped establish care ethics as a philosophical tradition that contrasts with the work of Enlightenment philosophers such as Immanuel Kant and John Locke. Instead of emphasising the more instrumental and rational elements of moral reasoning, care ethicists point to the relationality, interdependence and embeddedness of moral decisions (Williams, 2001). Regarding the gendered nature of such characteristics, a key debate has ensued as to the extent to which they are essentially feminine and/or feminist (the latter paying more explicit attention to structurally organised inequalities of power; e.g. Fotaki et al., 2020). In *The Reproduction of Mothering*, for example, Chodorow (1978) attempts a gendered explanation on the basis that girls tend to be more engaged with care than boys given that their mothers, rather than fathers, have long provided the majority of care within their family (and beyond). Critiquing this gendered dimension of care, many feminist scholars have therefore emphasised that care does not (and should not) lie only within the private domain (Noddings, 2003). It has to be more radically politicised and, ultimately, degendered (e.g. The Care Collective, 2020). It is also important to recognise, however, that most care ethics scholars do recognise the socially (rather than biologically) constructed gendered nature of care attributes. For instance, and despite later criticisms of her work, Gilligan emphasises that it is within a *patriarchal* framework, that care is understood

> as a feminine ethic. Within a *democratic* framework, care is a human ethic. A feminist ethic of care is a different voice within a patriarchal culture because it joins reason with emotion, mind with body, self with relationships, men with women, resisting the divisions that maintain a patriarchal order. (Gilligan, 2011, p. 22)

Accordingly, many authors acknowledge that the 'different voice' identified by Gilligan exists in all of us, albeit to a different extent (Juujärvia et al., 2010).

What are the implications for the (marketing) organisation? Despite underlying divides and differences (see Fotaki, 2019), feminist ethics scholars converge in recognising moral problems as conflicts of responsibilities in embedded, relational contexts rather than abstract conflicts of rights and justice between individuals and organisations. While traditional, more masculine approaches would therefore (at best) focus on 'fair' results, feminist perspectives emphasise social processes and the extent to which they leave space for subjective evaluations that require empathy, intuition, harmony and listening. Therefore, from a feminist ethic of care perspective, the main goal of the marketing organisation should be to avoid harm and maintain healthy (internal and external) relationships. From there, as Borgerson (2007) argues, feminist perspectives begin to point to some general organisational principles that in many ways extend beyond preoccupations concerned with 'gender' or 'care'. For instance, their focus on relationships, interdependence and active involvement is also evident in many other non-Western theories and on some intersectional approaches.

More recent applications of feminist care ethics to organisations have emphasised a variety of organisational aspects that have the potential to be more 'caring'. After all, as Fotaki et al. (2020) emphasise, organisations are essentially about relationships: 'work is conducted through relationships with co-workers, suppliers, clients, the users of services and other stakeholders' (p. 11). Any of these relationships is multi-faceted, subject to multiple demands and potentially conflicting care needs. For instance, focusing on organisational leadership, Nicholson and Kurucz (2019, p. 26) outline how a more care-oriented, relational approach envisions 'leadership as a social influence process through which coordination and change emerge, and in which primacy is placed on social processes of co-construction, rather than on the individuals involved'. Against a more common masculine notion of leadership as an individual (commonly a white man) rallying others towards their leader-generated vision and in line with care ethics, these authors propose a more relational, co-created leadership style that pays attention to complexity in organisations, and processes that can ensure mutual development and well-being. Similarly, Engster (2011) focuses on the relationship of organisations with their stakeholders, and applies a care-based perspective to outline more fully what it means to conduct business in a truly caring manner. Even in the area of 'design thinking' and innovation, Hamington (2019) sees potential for a more 'caring design' approach, one that recognises the significance of cooperation along the principles of empathy and enquiry.

Beyond such organisational aspects that are common across different sectors, it is also interesting to note that the word 'care' seems to have played a more prominent role within the *marketing* organisation. After all, as we note above, the marketing organisation remains more feminised with respect to both of its discursive and labour practices. 'Customer service' departments, for instance, were the first to change their name to 'customer care' (Folbre, 2014). Likewise, marketing communications commonly engage with themes of care giving and receiving, and as already discussed, carewashing is a practice that is widely observed in the industry. More profoundly perhaps, the so-called 'marketing orientation' is about identifying and satisfying customer (care) needs. In turn, internal marketing is about keeping employees happy and engaged. While this could imply that marketing organisations are more attuned to the importance of care in building internal and external relationships, somewhat ironically the opposite is rather more likely to be true. Care in marketing is viewed as a means to increasing profits rather than a means to increasing broader societal and environmental well-being. Instrumentalising care in this way may simply result in multiplying the caring demands of the members of the marketing organisation – not least in terms of the additional emotional and aesthetic labour discussed above – without caring for what else is happening in their everyday lives within or outside the organisation. Establishing a genuine care orientation in the organisation requires finding mechanisms that undo or invert such processes of worker burnout and exploitation (Fotaki et al., 2020).

Another interesting aspect of organisational care is that it defies easy measurement or operationalisation. As a notion, care incorporates numerous attributes, including attentive listening, patience, sympathising, recognition and acceptance, that do not subject themselves to mainstream organisational metrics. An interesting example here is the notion of a 'caring climate', itself understood as a distinct type of an organisation's overall 'ethical climate' or the type of 'work climate which guides ethical behaviour within organizations' (Fu and Deshpande, 2014, p. 340) and which is broken into professionalism, rules, instrumental, efficiency, independence and caring (Victor and Cullen, 1988). Measurement of the caring climate is restricted to standardised questions of 'friendship' and 'team interest' (Kao et al., 2014). These are in turn correlated with the positive outcomes of having a 'caring climate' such as job satisfaction, organisational commitment, worker withdrawal and job performance vis-à-vis the alternative working climates (Fu and Deshpande, 2014; Kao et al., 2014). As such, the notion of organisational care remains highly restrictive and instrumentalised. Interestingly, the notion of a 'caring climate' is rather more widely operationalised in education, occupational and sport psychology studies, understood for example as 'the extent to which individuals perceive a particular setting to be interpersonally inviting, safe, supportive, and able to provide the experience of being valued and respected' (Fry and Gano-Overway, 2010, p. 296) and measured with questions such as 'everyone is treated with kindness' (Newton et al., 2007). Even there, however, measures of care are context specific, focused on some specific qualities of the instructor–instructee relationship, and the effects these have on measures of performance. Measuring the qualities of care within and outside of the organisation is bound to remain far more elusive, reliant as they are on factors such as labour intensity, income, availability of resources and overall well-being.

More generally, then, care-based approaches are useful in raising a series of questions not only in relation to organisational rules or results, but also the more invisible everyday procedures, encounters and relationships. Despite their underlying differences and even potential danger in essentialising gender differences (Fotaki, 2019), the lens of care ethics is particularly powerful in asserting that gender equality is not only a question of outcomes but also of processes, and of both substance (e.g. attentiveness to mutual well-being) and surface (e.g. in the form of measurable organisational results, certifications, etc.). At the same time, it is wrong to assume that organisations, be they public or private, can care directly in the sense of mirroring human care–care relationships (Noddings, 2015). Rather, what they can do is to support the material and social conditions under which caring relations can prosper. Ultimately, a caring (marketing) organisation is one underpinned by such conditions, however elusive and indeed resistant to quantification and/or instrumentalisation these may be.

NOTES

1.   https://careersmart.org.uk/occupations/marketing-and-sales-directors
     https://careersmart.org.uk/occupations/equality/which-jobs-do-men-and
     -women-do-occupational-breakdown-gender
2.   https://business.linkedin.com/marketing-solutions/blog/linkedin-news/
     2021/gender-diversity-in-the-new-world-of-work
3   https://careersmart.org.uk/occupations/marketing-and-sales-directors

https://careersmart.org.uk/occupations/equality/which-jobs-do-men-and-women-do-occupational-breakdown-gender
4.   S&P Composite 1500 Index is a stock market index of US stocks made by Standard & Poor's.

7.   Can marketing be de-gendered?

The preceding six chapters have illustrated the myriad ways in which marketing is gendered and the often adverse impacts these may have on wider society. How can some of the imbalances and inequities we have identified be addressed? Now, in this concluding chapter we make some suggestions as well as flagging recent work that moves feminist debates in marketing forward. First, we reflect on current theorising around feminist solidarities and how their intersectional grounding influences our analyses of marketing and consumer research. Then we turn to the idea of demarketing and how this may open up new directions for feminist research. Finally, we come full circle and, having written much on gendering marketing, we end by envisioning what its de-gendering would look like.

FEMINIST SOLIDARITIES AND MARKETING

The recent backlash to the individualist emphasis of neoliberal feminism (Rottenberg, 2018), an iteration of feminism rooted in market logics (see Chapter 3), marks a significant turning point with the resurgence of feminist activism (Littler and Rottenberg, 2021). New solidarities have emerged to (once again) challenge socio-economic and political inequities. The Women's March, The Global Women's Strike, #metoo, #timesup and the Everyday Sexism Project are just some of the high-profile movements that have succeeded in mobilising large swathes of women. A key underpinning principle of feminist solidarity – itself a notion dating back to the writings of bell hooks in the 1980s (hooks, 1981) – is to unite women across traditional sociological categories of difference such as race, ethnicity, sexuality, religion and class in the fight for equality and the opposition to patriarchal power.

Intersectionality emerged during third-wave feminism as a powerful critique of second-wave thinking, especially in questioning white, middle-class women's domination of feminism along with the presumption that their group could speak for all women. Betty Friedan's (1963) construction of the bored housewife syndrome as a universal women's problem provoked a penetrating critique from hooks (1984). She high-lighted how Friedan ignored the many non-white and poor white women who would assist this middle-class model of womanhood to move into the public sphere. Hence, intersectionality is very much rooted in black feminist philosophy and identifies intersecting axes of oppression as those aspects of identity that lead to discrimination or marginalisation. As a principle, intersectionality enables us to make a more holistic analysis of how social categories can create a complex mix of disadvantages. Importantly, too, the relationship between categories is mutually constitutive and one category takes its meaning from its relation with another (black, woman, working class, lesbian, etc.). Being relational, intersectional identities are, therefore, always in process, shifting and changing in response to different contextual factors (Shields, 2008). Of course, many intersections bring advantages as well (white, male, heterosexual, and so forth) and the term 'privilege-checking', now in common parlance, refers to being reflexive about our taken-for-granted advantages and how these underpin our own viewpoints.

The whole point about feminist solidarity is for women to transcend markers of difference and to coalesce around common political aims. Yet this can be difficult to achieve. Recent critique by Alev Kuruoğlu (2022) reveals how knitting circles – as a form of craft-based activism challenging the devaluation of feminine labour and its absence from public spaces – exclude some women even while they encourage feminist solidarity. In the public imagination knitting remains a white woman's activity and black women are largely absent from its discourse. Often, therefore, they do not feel welcome in knitting spaces with some black women reporting experiences of micro-aggressions when they do participate.

In addition, marketing logics can work against the principle of feminist solidarities because they so often reinforce an individualist rather than a collectivist ethos. At its core, marketing adopts 'a divide and rule' approach that involves ever more finely honed market segmentation and targeting. This often results in perpetuating categories of difference to foster new market opportunities, especially in relation to sex differences (male/female/gay) as we have frequently shown throughout this book, but also in relation to the other identity markers that have burgeoned since the postmodern turn in the 1990s. Postmodernism's emphasis on lifestyles and 'hybrid consumption' for consumers diluted the issue of gender in social and political processes, suggesting as it did that no one variable has priority over other variables in an individual's make-up.

Identity politics, as popularly understood,[1] marked a significant shift from the activist feminist movements of the 1970s to what has sometimes been described as ludic or celebratory feminism; a feminism heavily mediated by the marketplace. Nike culture, for example, began targeting women during this period, appealing to a more authentic self that could be realised through exercise and thereby perceived as promoting feminist values. The brand's empowerment message played a pivotal role in encouraging women to become more physically active (Scott, 1992). Despite this, we need to remain sceptical because the focus of the message on individual satisfaction can be viewed as hindering collective efforts to challenge macro-level structural barriers to the progress of women. Indeed, this point remains highly relevant today, especially in relation to the digital world, as Sobande (2022) illustrates so powerfully in her analysis of the racist and sexist dynamics that structure black women's contemporary digital experiences. Her work reveals how marketers' co-optation of the black digital experience – particularly in the wake of the Black Lives Matter movement – not only undermines the communal potentials of black women's creative work, but also amplifies unequal power relations through its commodification of their work in digital spaces.

So, in the light of an increasing recognition that feminist socio-political aims may be stifled by individualising market mediation, it seems we are returning once again to the recognition that a wider feminist solidarity is required to effect structural change. Just how this principle will impact and influence marketing in the future remains to be seen, but we can say for sure that a decolonising perspective will play an important role in the future. Marketers will need to acknowledge local feminisms, particularly in relation to the Global South, as Ourahmoune and El Jurdi (2022) so emphatically affirm in their detailed analysis of feminist resistance in the Arab world. Often social marketing approaches encourage a 'white saviour' mindset by reinforcing the notion that women in the Global South lack agency. In contrast, revealing women to be at the forefront of a digital revolution in the MENA countries, Ourahmoune and El Jurdi argue the West's 'passive victims' tropes of Arab women are not helpful and prevent more nuanced understandings of the gender impediments they face. Specific local dynamics engender complex mixtures of consumption patterns that incorporate both emancipatory and ultra-modern Western-style consumer patterns.

A more positive view of marketing's potential role in feminist solidarities comes if we shift our focus from consumption to production and consider what Linda Scott (2020) terms the Double X Economy – an economy composed of women. A long-term proponent of women's economic empowerment, Scott packs her book on the topic, *The Double X Economy: The Epic Potential of Empowering Women*, with eye-watering statistics to bring home the gender inequities of the global economy and how much of women's work, whether it be household production or agricultural labour, is undervalued if, indeed, it is valued at all. Her core argument is that women share economic disadvantage when compared to their male counterparts and this holds true regardless of religion, ethnicity, class and race. Her message to policy makers and governments is simple: when women are economically empowered, communities benefit. Facilitating access to markets, at least within the current socio-economic system, is one way of furthering this end. However, there are many gender-based barriers to marketplace entry that must be overcome before this can happen, barriers that limit the resources available to women (e.g. finance, information, supply chain networks, and even time to focus solely on their enterprise, given the likelihood of them working a 'double shift'). To this end, and unpacking the conflation of patriarchy with capitalism, Scott argues that corporations have an important role in women's empowerment, especially in developing countries. This is especially evidenced in her work on the ground in Africa with Avon representatives who have successfully used the Avon sales and distribution networks to escape poverty and enhance their own sense of self-worth while enabling a better life for their families. Of course, Scott is not suggesting that businesses alone can achieve the requisite structural changes and her core message is that many macro-level aspects need to be addressed by policy makers and government. For example, a first priority for any economy, as Scott (2020, p. 169) highlights, is: 'to provide for the material needs of its members and to support the reproduction of the species … The ethic of the Double X Economy is to prioritize this provisioning.' In the discussions that follow we revisit some of the debates around the devaluing of 'women's work' and what this means in terms of marketing logics.

DEMARKETISING AND DEMARKETING FEMINISM

As we have seen, the history of feminist activism has been underpinned by widespread disbelief and suspicion as to the role of markets (and marketers) in a gender-equal world. This is despite the fact that, somewhat paradoxically, historic campaigns such as the one for 'wages for housework' (Federici, 1975) in many ways represented an attempt to recognise and give monetary value to care and social reproduction. However, their aim was to foreground the economic role of women's activity, not to give markets a more prominent role in care provisioning. Later iterations, such as the 'universal caregiver' (Fraser, 1994) and 'universal care' (The Care Collective, 2020) models, made that clearer by pointing out that it is down to broader political institutions and infrastructures, not markets, to facilitate everyone's care giving and receiving. For many progressive and eco-socialist feminists, markets do not have the capacity to radically address either gender inequalities or the largely feminised sectors of care and social reproduction. At the same time, some feminist activists and scholars have dubbed the concerns of anti-market feminists as 'commodification anxieties' (Nelson, 1999; Folbre and Nelson, 2000), in so far as they ignore cultural, institutional and legal conditions and regulations that can, under some circumstances, enable markets and marketing to advance feminist causes (e.g. Scott, 2020).

Notwithstanding the above, many concerns about the role of markets and marketing in a feminist and gender-equal world have been long-standing and difficult to rebut. The relatively more recent iterations of market and neoliberal feminism, as well the advent of femme-, pink- and carewashing, have further increased cynicism and revived a series of arguments as to why markets and feminism may often be incompatible.

First, it is axiomatic that markets allow or exclude entry on the basis of buying power. Although this has, in particular socio-historic moments, proved to be particularly liberating and empowering for groups that lacked other forms of cultural status and recognition (e.g. gay subcultures; Kates, 2002) it is also true that market exchanges are hardly ever done from positions of relative equal capacity. The fact that in many countries overall (Dorling, 2018) and gender-based (e.g. Fortin et al., 2017) income inequality continues to grow means that participation in markets remains fundamentally imbalanced. A related, more specific point to marketing practice, as noted earlier, is that consumer demand is commonly driven on the basis of segmentation and subjective preferences. Such strategies reproduce categories of difference and individualist logics that are incompatible with more collectivist and radically inclusive forms of feminist solidarity. Buying a queer brand, a feminist badge or supporting a cause-related marketing campaign (e.g. pink ribbon) may be a way of symbolically differentiating oneself from others yet it is common for such forms of activism (often dubbed as slacktivism) to stop there rather than pave the way for collective commitment and action in favour of gender justice. While the potential of such campaigns to resignify specific gendered practices and to engage with the politics of representation more broadly should not be dismissed, it is also true that such practices can be fully decoupled from the material and socio-economic reality of various feminist struggles.

Second, many feminist activists and scholars continue to emphasise that markets do not have the capacity to recognise and give value to many qualities that are culturally coded as feminine and thereby devalued. For instance, various kinds of service and care work are subject to non-market attributes such as empathy, attentive listening, compassion, commitment and so on that cannot be subjected to logics of instrumentalisation and quantification. As many feminist economists argue, most forms of care work and intimate labour further suffer from systemic devaluation, a 'cost disease' according to Razavi, 2007. That is, greater time efficiencies cannot be achieved in forms of labour when the time spent is often part of the activity and affects its overall quality (e.g. listening to someone's problems). Yet, their relative cost gets even higher as substantial efficiencies and economies of scale are achieved in other sectors of the economy (e.g. in the production of goods).

Third is the bigger picture questions around the types of subjectivities and ways of being that are cultivated through markets and marketing. There is no doubt that traditional non-market realms of life, from community relations to public spaces and goods such as healthcare and education, are increasingly subjected to the vocabulary of markets, free choice and consumerism (Massey, 2013). Such vocabulary builds on particular ideologies of independence, possessive and competitive individualism that are incompatible with more radical feminist ideals. Put differently, the kind of boardroom or 1 per cent feminism that is heavily criticised by eco-socialist feminists (Aruzza et al., 2019) is embraced not only in the workplace but also on the high street. As we illustrate in Chapter 5, evidence of possessive and competitive individualism is ubiquitous, from the burgeoning self-care industry to practices of intensive market-driven parenting, and from commercialised third spaces to customer-oriented health and educational institutions.

Similarly, at the level of marketing communications, we have already discussed attempts to portray corporate activities as feminist, LGBTQI+ positive and, more recently, caring. These are not only worrisome because of their alleged hypocrisy, they are also potentially problematic because they serve to legitimise the role of corporations as main actors in a variety of different forms of welfare and care provisioning. Unlike states and other non-market institutions, however, corporations are not democratically elected or governed. They are not obliged to adhere to feminist, caring and intersectional agendas even when these challenge the interests of their shareholders. Put differently, both individual-consumerist and corporate forms of charitable and voluntary giving progress on the ideological assumption that helping others and addressing social issues is an individual choice and therefore markets are the institution that best serves them (Tronto, 2013). Beyond the apparent democratic deficit that is normalised in this way – and the observation that both individuals and corporations tend to support those causes that are closest to their own interests (Tronto, 2013) – feminist perspectives would confront the very notion of individual choice and independence. In her most recent book, for example, Judith Butler (2020) emphasises that whilst liberal political thought assumes we come to this world as individuals, the opposite is true: 'each [of us] is dependent, or formed and sustained in relations of depending upon, and being depended upon' (p. 16).

On the basis of the above, the feminist agenda, broadly speaking, is set to retain a high level of suspicion about the role of markets and consumers in a gender-equal world. Interestingly, although the call for demarketising and re-collectivising many sectors of our everyday activity has been long-standing and understandably persistent (e.g. The Care Collective, 2020), the more specific role that can be played by demarketing – understood conventionally as 'marketing that deals with discouraging customers in general or a certain class of customers in particular on a temporary or permanent basis' (Kotler and Zaltman, 1971) – has been less understood. Somewhat paradoxically, then, marketing is in a unique position to drive the feminist agenda forward. It can, for instance, channel demand away from services and products that reproduce gender stereotypes, by demarketing stereotyped services and products, and by promoting gender-neutral alternatives. In addition, it can encourage the anti-consumption of products and services underpinned by gendered forms of injustice and exploitation (e.g. companies or countries of origin that are notorious for gender discrimination), in the same way that 'buy nothing' campaigns[2] are juxtaposed against heavily commercial events such as Black Friday. Furthermore, although demarketing can only address consumption rather than systems of production (Hall and Wood, 2021) and/or patriarchal exploitation, it can play a key role in broader processes of demarketisation, by unsettling consumerist logics in realms where they have proved to be hugely problematic, from healthcare and education to public services (Brown, 2015).

DIGITAL COMMONS

In the age of new digital technologies, big data and surveillance capitalism the role of gender and marketing is continuously evolving, raising new issues and reviving long-standing ones. For instance, the harsh realities of trolling, cyberstalking and revenge porn have tamed early optimism about the capacity of online feminist activism to bring about positive social change (Clark-Parsons, 2018). Furthermore, as we discuss in Chapter 2, the design of web technologies continues to reproduce gender stereotypes, and differential distributions of power and privilege more broadly. Feminist perspectives have also played a central role in questioning the value chain of digital production and consumption, from data mining to digital use and consumption of electricity, to disposal.

In response to such advancements, feminist activists and scholars have begun to engage with notions of 'digital commons' as an alternative to privatised digital production and consumption. This is not surprising given that, as Sylvia Federici (2012, p. 143) puts it, 'historically and in our time, women have depended more than men on access to communal resources, and have been most committed to their defence'. Central to such a feminist agenda is also the idea of collaborative production through collectively owned and managed platforms, what is also known as 'platform co-operativism' – as a counter proposal to capitalist innovations such as Facebook, YouTube, Uber and Airbnb. Fairbnb, for example, is an ethical home sharing site that directly challenges Airbnb and focuses instead on sustainable tourism that gives resources back to the local community. In terms of digital consumption and co-production, feminist perspectives also emphasise the need for safe online spaces that counter the growth of online harassment and sexism (Jane, 2014). There are currently many feminist groups on social media that are particularly popular because members can be assured of being safe to express their views without fear of mockery or denigration. Additionally, privacy settings can be useful in terms of limiting access or allowing bloggers to remain invisible, therefore functioning as a 'networked counterpublic' (Clark-Parsons, 2018). One such counterpublic is Slutwalk, a transnational feminist movement against sexual violence and rape culture, which works to change attitudes around victim blaming and which uses social networking sites to circulate women's testimonies and coordinate cyberactions.

Feminist concerns have also been raised in response to the rise of big data and algorithmic marketing. Beyond broader questions around how information is created, manipulated and valorised by digital marketers (Darmody and Zwick, 2020), 'data feminists' (Ignazio and Klein, 2020) have begun to emphasise how big data and data science are overwhelmingly white, male and techno-heroic. Ignazio and Klein's collaborative project focuses on challenging and changing the hierarchical classification systems that feed into data science by following intersectional feminist principles such as elevating emotion and embodiment, rethinking binaries, embracing pluralism and considering the context of social relations. Interestingly, such ideas have already been embraced by digital marketers, or so it seems. Procter & Gamble's newest campaign for its Olay skincare brand is titled #Decodethebias, referring to the observation that the digital ecosystem 'is biased against minority demographics, particularly women of color' (Hiken, 2021). The campaign aims to address this by sending 1,000 girls of colour to the organisation's 'code camp'. Nonetheless, as we discuss in Chapter 5, such promotions of inclusivity and female empowerment can also be viewed as the latest manifestations of femmewashing and carewashing. Whether they represent a genuine step towards feminist marketing remains an open question.

FEMINIST FUTURES IN MARKETING

In this final section we return to the subject of feminist solidarities and speculate on the potential of feminist social movements to play a role in de-gendering marketing. As we have frequently highlighted throughout this book, feminist messages are often co-opted by corporations and reduced by marketers to individualising empowerment missives that do not support, or may even prevent, the mobilisation of a more collective ethos required to bring about structural change. Yet, as we have also tried to show, we cannot automatically judge corporate interventions as bad, even in the case of obvious greenwashing: sometimes it is the outcome rather than the intention that matters; and often outcomes can only be judged in the longer term. There are both pros and cons underpinning what Otnes and Fischer (2022) term 'feminist brands', a list that includes feminist social movements themselves that employ branding tactics to increase awareness of their causes. As regards the latter, for example, the use of branding may successfully increase levels of economic and human support for a movement. In turn, this may result in the movement's mainstreaming, however, and the privileging of white, cis-feminists (Otnes and Fischer, 2022).

Hence, a pertinent challenge for future feminist scholarship in marketing is the development of more nuanced and sophisticated understandings of the intricate relationship between markets, consumption and gender. Current research (both in marketing and across other disciplines) rarely moves beyond strictly celebratory or dystopian accounts, yet it is probably the case that markets are relatively more effective in redressing at least some forms of gender injustice (e.g. Scott, 2020), under specific conditions, and less so for others (e.g. Steinfield, 2021).

Certainly, evidence shows that feminist social movements are adapting to the current dominance of corporate governance and seeking to maximise opportunities as gender issues move to the top of Corporate Social Responsibility (CSR) agendas (Grosser and McCarthy, 2019). Accordingly, despite CSR initiatives contributing heavily to the neoliberalisation of feminism they also constitute a new site for its contestation. Feminist social movements are furthering their own struggles, not just through adversorial campaigns but also by establishing collaborative partnerships to influence decision-making around corporate codes of practice and diversity strategising (Grosser and McCarthy, 2019). For example, Women Working Worldwide, a British voluntary organisation advocating for women workers in global supply chains has developed strategic links with major brands such as Tesco and Marks & Spencer. Notably, this women's organisation is also a founder member of the Ethical Trading Initiative (ETI) driving responsible business practices through collaborative action between grassroots NGOs, trade unions and corporations. An impressive list of brands – including The Body Shop, Sainsbury's, ASOS and The White Company, to name but a few – are members of the ETI. Should this be viewed as appropriation and co-optation of feminist ideals by corporate interests for the purposes of positive publicity and societal legitimation? Or, more optimistically, should it be viewed as part of a longer multi-stakeholder, multi-level intervention that may effectively transmute radical feminist ideas into mainstream discourse and practice?

We have frequently illustrated how marketing is closely intertwined with CSR, especially in terms of reputational effects on brand image, as well as the various possibilities for cause-related promotional tie-ins. In addition, the marketing role traditionally coordinates internal business functions, customers and other stakeholders in order to maintain a positive, overarching image for an organisation. Marketers are thus well placed to assist in creating the sense of wider community that CSR efforts drive and to make critical interventions that avoid greenwashing. Further research into these dynamics by feminist marketing academics could provide many fruitful insights, particularly in relation to how feminist allies within organisations can support the causes of feminist social movements without their translation into a more muted form of neoliberal feminism. In other words, how movement agendas can retain their collective momentum to influence policy making. There is also the possibility of feminist marketers mobilising collective responses from women through cause-related campaigns such as the brand Pampers' ongoing partnership with UNICEF's vaccination programme for maternal and neo-natal tetanus (e.g. the purchase of one pack of Pampers nappies equals the provision of one vaccine). This sponsorship supports the work that UNICEF is doing with national and local governments to deliver these tetanus vaccinations. No one can deny the effectiveness of this campaign in both alleviating suffering on the ground and raising wide awareness of the cause amongst a target audience likely to be sympathetic (i.e. young mothers). At the same time, and quite rightly, the campaign has been heavily criticised for its postcolonial and individualising tropes that obscure from deeply entrenched North–South power dynamics and the systemic causes of global poverty (Hawkins, 2011).

Without a doubt the relationship between advocates and marketers/ corporations presents a complex picture, full of fluctuating power dynamics that elude our current understanding. More nuanced perspectives are steadily emerging, however, such as Steinfield's (2021) scrutiny of the non-human as well as human elements in those dynamics and her unravelling of historical entanglements. Using her own experiences of researching Walmart's Empowering Women Together (EWT) initiative, Steinfield elucidates the role of 'things' in determining outcomes, despite the good intentions of all involved. In this instance, non-human aspects such as corporate reports, audits and standards, with their focus on economic measurements, drove certain corporate outcomes while silencing other, more unquantifiable ones determined by women's caring and reproductive roles. Ultimately such measures impeded women's organisational advancement. A key role for feminist marketers is therefore to untangle strategic corporate framings and ensure that they do not undermine the objectives of partner activist groups.

This reminds us that we still have much to learn (let alone change) about the broader economic, cultural and legal conditions that can facilitate a more redistributive and welfarist role of markets and marketing while promoting feminist ideals and values. Most certainly, this is a highly challenging and complicated task but arguably the need to unpack this complexity has never been more pertinent. The future of marketing is unlikely to be fully de-gendered, but our hope is that feminist activists and scholars will play a much greater role in shaping it.

NOTES

1. But see e.g. https://holbergprisen.no/en/2021-holberg-debate-identity-politics -and-culture-wars
2. For example, https://www.buynothingday.co.uk/

References

Adam, A. (2003), 'Hacking into hacking: Gender and the hacker phenomenon', *ACM SIGCAS Computers and Society*, **33** (4), 3.

Ahl, H. (2006), 'Why research on women entrepreneurs needs new direction', *Entrepreneurship Theory and Practice,* **30** (5), 595–621.

Ajzen, I. (1991), 'The theory of planned behaviour', *Organizational Behavior and Human Decision Processes*, **50** (2), 179–211.

Akestam, N., S. Rosengren and M. Dahlen (2017), 'Advertising "like a girl": Toward a better understanding of "femvertising" and its effects', *Psychology & Marketing*, **34** (8), 795–806.

Alexander, M., M. Burt and A. Collinson (1995), 'Big talk, small talk: BT's strategic use of semiotics in planning its current advertising', *Journal of the Market Research Society*, **37** (2), 91–102.

Allen, S. (2018), 'Why Coke's non-binary superbowl moment mattered', *Daily Beast*, 5 February, accessed 4 November 2020 at www.thedailybeast.com/why-cokes-non-binary-super-bowl-moment-mattered

Alvesson, M. (1998), 'Gender relations and identity at work: A case study of masculinities and femininities in an advertising agency', *Human Relations,* **51**, 969–1005.

Anciaux, A. (2020), 'A digital redefinition of the pornography industries', in E. George (ed.), *Digitalization of Society and Socio-Political Issues 1: Digital, Communication, and Culture*, New Jersey: John Wiley & Sons, pp. 126–133.

Arnold, L. (2015), 'Lilian Vernon, queen of mail-order catalogs, dies at 88', *Washington Post*, 15 December.

Arnould, E. J. and C. J. Thompson (2015), 'Introduction: Consumer culture theory: Ten years gone (and beyond)', in A. E. Thyroff, J. B. Murray and R. W. Belk (eds), *Consumer Culture Theory: Research in Consumer Behavior Vol. 17*, London: Sage, pp. 1–21.

Arruzza, C., T. Bhattacharya and N. Fraser (2019), *Feminism For the 99 Percent. A Manifesto*, London and New York: Verso Books.

Banet-Weiser, S. (2018), *Empowered: Popular Feminism and Popular Misogyny*, Durham, NC: Duke University Press.

Banet-Weiser, S. and K. M. Miltner, (2016), '# MasculinitySoFragile: Culture, structure, and networked misogyny', *Feminist Media Studies*, **16** (1), 171–174.

Barad, K. (2003), 'Posthumanist performativity: Toward an understanding of how matter comes to matter', *Signs: Journal of Women in Culture and Society,* **28** (3), 801–831.

Bareket, O., R. Kahalon, N. Shnabel and P. Glick (2018), 'The Madonna–whore dichotomy: Men who perceive women's nurturance and sexuality as mutually exclusive endorse patriarchy and show lower relationship satisfaction', *Sex Roles: A Journal of Research*, **79** (9–10), 519–532.

BBC News (2016), 'Price differences for men and women "astonishing"', accessed 18 November 2021 at www.bbc.co.uk/news/newsbeat-35359541

BBC News (2020), 'Madame C J Walker: "An Inspiration to us all"', accessed 4 November 2021 at www.bbc.co.uk/news/business-52130592

Beauvoir, S. de (1949), *Le Deuxieme Sexe*, Paris: Editions Gallimard.

Beery, A. T. (1972), 'The feminist movement; attitudes behavior and potential', in M. Venkatesan (ed.), *Proceedings of the Third Annual Conference of the Association for Consumer Research*, Chicago, IL: Association for Consumer Research, pp. 446–455.

Belkaoui, A. and J. Belkaoui (1976), 'A comparative analysis of the roles portrayed by women in print advertisements: 1958, 1970, 1972', *Journal of Marketing Research*, **12** (2), 168–172.

Bell, P. and M. Milic (2002), 'Goffman's gender advertisements revisited: Combining content analysis with semiotic analysis', *Visual Communication*, **1** (2), 203–222.

Benioff, M. and K. Southwick (2004), *Compassionate Capitalism: How Corporations Can Make Doing Good an Integral Part of Doing Well*, Franklin Lakes, NJ: Career Press.

Berger, J. (1972), *Ways of Seeing*, New York: Penguin Books.

Bien-Aimé, T. (2020), 'The pornography industry's aggressive marketing practices explained', accessed 18 November at www.endsexualexploitation.org/articles/the-pornography-industrys-aggressive-marketing-tactics-explained

Black, J. (2006), 'War, women and accounting: Female staff in the UK Army Pay Department offices, 1914–1920', *Accounting, Business & Financial History*, **16** (2), 195–218.

Boltanski, L. and E. Chiapello (2007), *The New Spirit of Capitalism*, London: Verso Books.

Bondurant, B. (2013), 'The privatization of prisons and prisoner healthcare: Addressing the extent of prisoners' right to healthcare', *New England Journal on Criminal and Civil Confinement*, **39** (2), 407–426.

Bordo, S. (1993), *Unbearable Weight: Feminism, Western Culture, and the Body*, Berkeley: University of California Press.

Borgerson, J. L. (2007), 'On the harmony of feminist ethics and business ethics', *Business and Society Review*, **112** (4), 477–509.

Borgerson, J. L, J. E. Schroeder, B. Blomberg and E. Thorssén (2006), 'The gay family in the ad: Consumer responses to non-traditional families in marketing communications', *Journal of Marketing Management*, **22** (9–10), 955–978.

Bowman, M. (2004), 'Presidential address given to the Folklore society, March 2004: Procession and possession in Glastonbury: Continuity, change and the manipulation of tradition', *Folklore*, **115** (3), 273–285.

Bradley, M. Z. (1982), *The Mists of Avalon*, New York: Ballantine Books.

Braidotti, R. (1994), *Nomadic Subjects: Embodiment and Sexual Difference in Contemporary Feminist Theory*, New York: Columbia University Press.

Brickell, C. (2003), 'Performativity or performance? Clarifications in the sociology of gender', *New Zealand Sociology*, **18** (2), 158–178.

Bristor, J. M. and E. Fischer (1993), 'Feminist thought: Implications for consumer research', *Journal of Consumer Research*, **19** (4), 518–536.

Broadbent, J. and L. Kirkham (2008), 'Glass ceilings, glass cliffs or new worlds? Revisiting gender and accounting', *Accounting, Auditing & Accountability Journal*, **21** (4), 465–473.

Brown, W. (2015), *Undoing the Demos: Neoliberalism's Stealth Revolution*, Cambridge, MA: The MIT Press.

Brownlie, D. and P. Hewer (2007), 'Prime beef cuts: Culinary images for thinking "men"', *Consumption, Markets and Culture*, **10** (3), 229–250.

Bruckman, A. S. (1993), 'Gender swapping on the Internet', paper presented at Internet Society Conference (INET93), San Francisco, CA, August.

Burns, K. (1999), *Colonial Habits: Convents and the Spiritual Economy of Cuzco, Peru*, Durham, NC: Duke University Press.

Burt, T. (2021), 'How women in marketing are advancing in the new world of work', *Marketing Solutions* blog, 29 June, accessed 1 December 2021 at www.business.linkedin.com/marketing-solutions/blog/linkedin-news/2021/gender-diversity-in-the-new-world-of-work

Business Matters (2020), '5 lessons that the pornographic industry can teach online marketing', accessed 18 November 2021 at www.bmmagazine.co.uk/in-business/5-lessons-the-pornographic-industry-to-online-marketing

Butler, J. (1990), *Gender Trouble: Feminism and the Subversion of Identity*, New York: Routledge.

Butler, J. (1993), *Bodies That Matter: On the Discursive Limits of 'Sex'*, New York: Routledge.

Butler, J. (2004), *Precarious Life: The Powers of Mourning and Violence*, London: Verso Books.

Butler, J. (2020), *The Force of Nonviolence: An Ethico-Political Bind*, London and New York: Verso Books.

Butler, J., P. Osbourne and L. Segal (1994), 'Gender as performance: An interview with Judith Butler', *Radical Philosophy*, **67** (summer), 32–39.

Calas, M. and L. Smircich (1991), 'Voicing seduction to silence leadership', *Organisation Studies*, **12** (4), 567–602.

Cappellini, B., D. Marshall and E. Parsons (eds) (2016), *The Practice of the Meal: Food, Families and the Market Place*, London: Routledge.

Catterall, M., P. Maclaran and L. Stevens (eds) (2000), *Marketing and Feminism: Current Issues and Research*, London: Routledge.

Catterall, M., P. Maclaran and L. Stevens (2005), 'Postmodern paralysis: The critical impasse in feminist perspectives on consumers', *Journal of Marketing Management*, **21** (5/6), 489–504.

Chatterjee, D. and N. Monroe (2020), 'Marketing beyond the gender binary', accessed 18 November 2021 at www.sloanreview.mit.edu/article/marketing-beyond-the-gender-binary

Chatzidakis, A. (2022), 'Anti-consumption and the current crisis of care', in M. A. Lee and H. Cherrier (eds), *The Handbook of Anti-Consumption Research*, Routledge.

Chatzidakis, A. and J. Littler (2022), 'An anatomy of carewashing: Corporate branding and the commodification of care during Covid-19', *International Journal of Cultural Studies*, forthcoming.

Chatzidakis, A. and P. Maclaran (2020), 'Gendering consumer ethics', *International Journal of Consumer Studies*, **44** (4), 316–327.

Chatzidakis, A., P. Maclaran and A. Bradshaw (2012), 'Heterotopian space and the utopics of ethical and green consumption', *Journal of Marketing Management*, **28** (3–4), 494–515.

Chatzidakis, A., J. Hakim, J. Littler, C. Rottenberg and L. Segal (2020), 'From carewashing to radical care: The discursive explosions of care during Covid-19', *Feminist Media Studies*, **20** (6), 889–895.

Chen, C. P., A. Davies and R. Elliott (2002), 'Limits to ludic gaps: Gender and identity in a different cultural context', in P. Maclaran and E. Tissier-Desbordes (eds), *Proceedings of the Sixth Gender, Marketing and Consumer Behavior Conference*, pp. 69–84.

Chodorow, N. (1978), *The Reproduction of Mothering*, Berkeley: University of California Press.

Ciancanelli, P., S. Gallhofer, C. Humphrey and L. Kirkham (1990), 'Gender and accountancy: Some evidence from the UK', *Critical Perspectives on Accounting*, **1** (2), 117–144.

Clark-Parsons, R. (2018), 'Building a digital girl army: The cultivation of feminist safe spaces online', *New Media and Society*, **20** (6), 2125–2144.

Clifford, M. J. (2003), 'Helena Rubinstein's beauty salons, fashion, and modernist display', *Winterthur Portfolio*, **38** (2–3), 83–108.

Cockburn, C. (1997), 'Domestic technologies: Cinderella and the engineers', *Women's Studies International Forum*, **20** (3), 361–371.

Cockburn, C. and S. Omrod (1993), *Gender and Technology in the Making*, London: Sage.

Connell, R. W. and J. W. Messerschmidt (2005), 'Hegemonic masculinity: Rethinking the concept', *Gender & Society*, **19** (6), 829–859.

Cooke, B. (1999), 'Writing the Left out of management theory: The historiography of the management of change', *Organization*, **6** (1), 81–105.

Cooper, B. (2000), '"Chick Flicks" as feminist texts: The appropriation of the male gaze in Thelma and Louise', *Women's Studies in Communication*, **23** (3), 277–306.

Cornell, D. (2004), 'Pornography's temptation', *FGS–Freiburger Zeitschrift fur GeschlechterStudien*, **10** (2), 15–16.

Costa, J. A. (ed.) (1991), *Proceedings of the First Conference on Gender, Marketing and Consumer Behaviour*, Salt Lake City: University of Utah Printing Service.

Courtney, A. E. and T. W. Whipple (1983), *Sex Stereotyping in Advertising*, Lexington, MA: Lexington Books.

Cova, B., R. V. Kozinets and A. Shankar (eds) (2007), *Consumer Tribes*, London: Routledge.

Crane, A., D. Matten, S. Glozer and L. Spence (2019), *Business Ethics: Managing Corporate Citizenship and Sustainability in the Age of Globalization*, Oxford: Oxford University Press.

Criado Perez, C. (2019), *Invisible Women: Exposing Data Bias in a World Designed for Men*, London: Vintage.

Cross, T. (2019), 'Did Gillette's "The best men can be" campaign succeed? Here's what the data said', accessed 8 November 2021 at www.videoweek.com/2019/01/17/did-gillettes-the-best-men-can-be-campaign-succeed-heres-what-the-data-said

Darmody, A. and D. Zwick (2020), 'Manipulate to empower: Hyper-relevance and the contradictions of marketing in the age of surveillance capitalism', *Big Data & Society*, **7** (1), DOI: 10.1177/2053951720904112.

Dasu, S. and R. B. Chase (2010), 'Designing the soft side of customer service', *MIT Sloan Management Review*, **52** (1), 33–39.

Davies, A., P. Maclaran and E. Tissiers-Desbordes (2015), 'Confronting the abject in a retail servicescape', *Journal of Macromarketing*, **35** (1), 135–136.

Davis, J. F. (2013), 'Realizing marketplace opportunity: How research on the black consumer market influenced mainstream marketers, 1920–1970', *Journal of Historical Research in Marketing*, **5** (4), 471–493.

Davis, J. F. (2016), *Pioneering African-American Women in the Advertising Business: Biographies of MAD Black WOMEN*, London and New York: Routledge.

Davis, J. F. (2018), 'Selling whiteness? – A critical review of the literature on marketing and racism', *Journal of Marketing Management*, **34** (1–2), 134–177.

Davis, J. F. (2021), 'Marketing's hidden figures: Black women leaders in advertising', in P. Maclaran, L. Stevens and O. Kravets (eds), *The Routledge Companion to Marketing and Feminism*, London: Routledge, pp. 45–58.

Davis, K. (ed.) (1997), *Embodied Practices: Feminist Perspectives on the Body*, London: Sage.

Deem, R. (2003), 'Gender, organizational cultures and the practices of manager academics in UK universities', *Gender, Work and Organizations*, **10** (2), 239–259.

Dehaene, M. and L. de Cauter (2008), *Heterotopia and the City: Public Space in a Postcivil Society*, London: Routledge.

Desmond, J. (1997), 'Marketing and the war machine', *Marketing Intelligence and Planning*, **15** (7), 338–351.

Diamond, L. M. (2020), 'Gender fluidity and nonbinary gender identities among children and adolescents', *Child Development Perspectives*, **14** (2), 110–115.

Dines, G. (2010), *Pornland: How Porn has Hijacked our Sexuality*, Boston, MA: Beacon Press.

Dion, D. and S. Borraz (2017), 'Managing status: How luxury brands shape class subjectivities in the service encounter', *Journal of Marketing*, **81** (5), 67–85.

Dobscha, S. (1993), 'Women and the environment: Applying ecofeminism to environmentally-related consumption', *Advances in Consumer Research*, **20** (1), 36–40.

Dobscha, S. and J. L. Ozanne, (2000), 'Marketing and the divided self: Healing the nature/woman separation', in M. Catterall, P. Maclaran and L. Stevens (eds), *Marketing and Feminism: Current Issues and Research,* London: Routledge, pp. 239–254.

Dobscha, S. and J. L. Ozanne (2001), 'An ecofeminist analysis of environmentally sensitive women: Qualitative findings on the emancipatory potential of an ecological life', *Journal of Public Policy and Marketing*, **20** (2), 201–214.

Dobscha, S. and A. Prothero (2022), '"One, two, three, four, what are we fighting for?": Deconstructing climate crisis war messaging metaphors using ecofeminism', in P. Maclaran, L. Stevens and O. Kravets (eds), *The Routledge Companion to Marketing and Feminism*, London: Routledge, pp. 90–101.

Dorling, D. (2018), *Peak Inequality: Britain's Ticking Time Bomb*, Bristol: Policy Press.

Dowling, E. (2020), *The Care Crisis: What Caused It and How Can We End It?*, London: Verso Books.

Downey, G. L. and J. A. Lucena (1995), 'Engineering Studies', in S. Jasanoff, G. E. Markle, J. C. Petersen and T. Pinch (eds), *Handbook of Science and Technology Studies*, Thousand Oaks, CA: Sage, pp. 167–188.

Downey, H. (2016), 'Poetic inquiry, consumer vulnerability: Realities of quadriplegia', *Journal of Marketing Management*, **32** (3–4), 357–364.

Drakett, J., B. Rickett, K. Day and K. Milnes, (2018), 'Old jokes, new media – Online sexism and constructions of gender in internet memes', *Feminism and Psychology*, **28** (1), 109–127.

Drenten, J., L. Gurrieri and M. Tyler (2020), 'Sexualized labour in digital culture: Instagram influencers, porn chic and the monetization of attention', *Gender, Work and Organization*, **27** (1), 41–66.

Drenten, J., R. Harrison and N. Pendarvis (2019), 'Video gaming as a gendered pursuit', in S. Dobscha (ed.), *Handbook of Research on Gender and Marketing*, Cheltenham, UK and Northampton, MA: Edward Elgar Publishing, pp. 28–44.

Duffy, K., P. Hancock and M. Tyler (2017), 'Still red hot? Post-feminism and gender subjectivity in the airline industry', *Gender, Work and Organization*, **24** (3), 260–273.

Durepos, G., A. McKinlay and S. Taylor (2017), 'Narrating histories of women at work: Archives, stories, and the promise of feminism', *Business History*, **59** (8), 1261–1279.

Dworkin, A. (1981), *Pornography: Men Possessing Women*, New York: Perigree.

Eaubonne, F. d' (1994), 'The time of Ecofeminism', in C. Merchant (ed.), trans. R. Hottell, *Ecology*, Atlantic Highlands, NJ: Humanities Press, pp. 174–197.

Elias, A., R. Gill and C. Scharff (2017), 'Aesthetic labour: Beauty politics in neoliberalism', in A. Elias, R. Gill and C. Scharff (eds), *Aesthetic Labour: Beauty Politics in Neoliberalism*, London: Palgrave Macmillan, pp. 3–49.

Eller, C. (2000), *The Myth of Matriarchal Prehistory: Why an Invented Past Won't Give Women a Future*, Boston, MA: Beacon Press.

Elmore, K. C. and M. Luna-Lucero (2017), 'Light bulbs or seeds? How metaphors for ideas influence judgments about genius', *Social Psychological and Personality Science*, **8** (2), 200–208.

Engster, D. (2011), 'Care ethics and stakeholder theory', in M. Hamington and M. Sander-Staudt (eds), *Applying Care Ethics to Business*, Dordrecht: Springer, pp. 93–110.

Evans, C. and L. Gamman (1995), 'The gaze revisited, or reviewing queer viewing', in P. Burston, and C. Richardson (eds), *A Queer Romance, Lesbians, Gay Men and Popular Culture*, London and New York: Routledge, pp. 12–61.

Evans, C. and N. Rumens (2020), 'Gender inequality and the professionalisation of accountancy in the UK from 1870 to the interwar years', *Business History*, forthcoming, DOI: 10.1080/00076791.2020.1763958.

Farris, S. R. and S. Marchetti (2017), 'From the commodification to the corporatization of care: European perspectives and debates', *Social Politics: International Studies in Gender, State and Society*, **24** (2), 109–131.

Farris, S and C. Rottenberg (2017), 'Introduction: Righting feminism', *New Formations: A Journal of Culture/Theory/Politics*, **91**, 5–1.

Faugoo, D. (2011), 'The advancement of women to top management positions in the human resource management domain: A time for change?', *International Journal of Business and Social Science*, **2** (20), 195–202.

Faulkner, W. (2001), 'The technology question in feminism: A view from feminist technology studies', *Women's Studies International Quarterly*, **24** (1), 79–95.

Federici, S. (1975), *Wages Against Housework*, Bristol: Falling Wall Press.

Federici, S. (2012), *Revolution at Point Zero: Housework, Reproduction, and Feminist Struggle*, Oakland, CA and Brooklyn, NY: PM Press and Autonomedia: Common Notions.

Fennell, D. A. (2012), *Tourism and Animal Ethics*, London: Routledge.

Fennell, D. A. (2015), 'The status of animal ethics research in tourism: A review of theory', in K. Markwell (ed.), *Animals and Tourism: Understanding Diverse Relationships*, Bristol: Channel View, pp. 27–43.

Fischer, E. (2000), 'A postmodern analysis of the implications of the discourse of mass customisation for marginalised and prized consumers', in M. Catterall, P. Maclaran and L. Stevens (eds), *Marketing and Feminism: Current Issues and Research*, London: Routledge, pp. 220–238.

Fischer, E. and J. Bristor (1994), 'A feminist poststructuralist analysis of the rhetoric of marketing relationships', *International Journal of Research in Marketing*, **11**, 317–331.

Folbre, N. (2014), *Who Cares? A Feminist Critique of the Care Economy*, New York: Rosa Luxemburg Stiftung.

Folbre, N. and J. Nelson (2000), 'For love or money – or both?', *Journal of Economic Perspectives*, **14** (4), 123–140.

Fortin, N. M., B. Bell and M. Böhm, (2017), 'Top earnings inequality and the gender pay gap: Canada, Sweden, and the United Kingdom', *Labour Economics*, **47**, 107–123.

Fotaki, M. (2019), 'Feminist ethics: Embodied relationality as a normative guide for management and organizations', in C. Neesham and R. Macklin (eds), *Handbook of Philosophy of Management*, New York: Springer, pp. 1–20.

Fotaki, M., G. Islam and A. Antoni (2020), *Business Ethics and Care in Organizations*, London: Routledge.

Foucault, M. (1977), *Discipline and Punishment*, trans. A. Sheridan, New York: Vintage Books.

Foucault, M. (1986), 'Of other spaces', *Diacritics*, **16** (1), 22–27.

Fournier, S., S. Dobscha and D. G. Mick (1998), 'Preventing the premature death of relationship marketing', *Harvard Business Review*, **76** (1), 42–51.

Fox, M. F., D. G. Johnson and S. V. Rosser (2006), *Women, Gender and Technology*, Urbana: University of Illinois Press.

Francis, T. and F. Hoefel (2018), '"True Gen": Generation Z and its implications for companies', accessed 18 November 2021 at www.mckinsey.com/industries/consumer-packaged-goods/our-insights/true-gen-generation-z-and-its-implications-for-companies

Fraser, N. (1994). 'After the family wage: Gender equity and the welfare state', *Political Theory*, **22** (4), 591–618.

Fraser, N. (2009), 'Social justice in the age of identity politics', in G. L. Henderson and M. Waterstone (eds), *Geographic Thought: A Praxis Perspective*, Routledge, pp. 72–91.

Fraser, N. (2013), *Fortunes of Feminism: From State-Managed Capitalism to Neoliberal Crisis*, London: Verso Books.

Fraser, N. (2016a), 'Capitalism's crisis of care', *Dissent*, **63** (4), 30–37.

Fraser, N. (2016b), 'Contradictions of capital and care', *New Left Review*, **100**, 99–117.

Fraser, N. and A. Honneth (2003), *Redistribution or Recognition: A Politicophilosophical Exchange*, London: Verso Books.

Frederick, C. (1929), *Selling Mrs Consumer*, New York: The Business Bourse.

Friedan, B. (1963), *The Feminine Mystique*, New York: W. W. Norton.

Fry, M. D. and L. A. Gano-Overway (2010), 'Exploring the contribution of the caring climate to the youth sport experience', *Journal of Applied Sport Psychology*, **22** (3), 294–304.

Fu, W. and S. P. Deshpande (2014), 'The impact of caring climate, job satisfaction, and organizational commitment on job performance of employees in a China's insurance company', *Journal of Business Ethics*, **124** (2), 339–349.

Gaard, G. (1993), 'Living interconnections with animals and nature', in G. Gaard (ed.), *Ecofeminism: Women, Animals, Nature*, Philadelphia, PA: Temple University Press, pp. 1–12.

Gamber, W. (1998), 'A gendered enterprise: Placing nineteenth-century business-women in history', *Business History Review*, **72** (2), 188–218.

Gamman, L. and M. Marshment (1988), *The Female Gaze: Women Viewers of Pop Culture*, London: Women's Press.

Garcia-Rada, X., M. Steffel, E. F. Williams and M. I. Norton (2021), 'Consumers value effort over ease when caring for close others', *Journal of Consumer Research* (forthcoming).

Gentry, J. and R. Harrison (2010), 'Is advertising a barrier to male movement toward gender change?', *Marketing Theory*, **10** (1), 74–96.

Getchell, K. M. and L. S. Beitelspacher (2020), 'Better marketing for female marketers: Gendered language in the Forbes CMO List', *Business Horizons*, **63** (5), 607–617.

Gherardi, S. (1995), *Gender, Symbolism and Organisational Cultures*, London: Sage.

Gilbert, J. (2013), *Common Ground: Democracy and Collectivity in an Age of Individualism*, London: Pluto Press.

Gill, R. (2008), 'Empowerment/sexism: Figuring female sexual agency in contemporary advertising', *Feminism and Psychology*, **18** (1), 35–60.

Gilligan, C. (1982), *In a Different Voice: Psychological Theory and Women's Development*, Cambridge, MA: Harvard University Press.

Gilligan, C. (2011), *Joining the Resistance*, Malden, MA: Polity Press.

Goffman, E. (1956), *The Presentation of Self in Everyday Life*, New York: Anchor Books.

Goffman, E. (1979), *Gender Advertisements*, London: Macmillan.

Goffman, E. (1986), *Frame Analysis*, Boston, MA: Northeastern University Press.

Gorbatch, A. (2019), 'Pornhub case study: 5 marketing steps that made it', accessed 18 November 2021 at www.awario.com/blog/pornhub-case-study -marketing

Grosser, K. and L. McCarthy (2019), 'Imagining new feminist futures: How feminist social movements contest the neoliberalization of feminism in an increasingly corporate-dominated world', *Gender, Work and Organization*, **26** (8), 1100–1116.

Grosz, E. (1994), *Volatile Bodies: Toward a Corporeal Feminism*, Bloomington: Indiana University Press.

Hacker, S. (1989), *Pleasure, Power and Technology: Some Tales of Gender, Engineering and the Cooperative Workplace*, Boston, MA: Unwin Hyman.

Hall, C. M. and K. J. Wood (2021), 'Demarketing tourism for sustainability: Degrowing tourism or moving the deckchairs on the Titanic?', *Sustainability*, **13** (3), 1585.

Hamad, R. (2020), *White Tears Brown Scars: How White Feminism Betrays Women of Colour*, Hachette UK.

Hamilton, K., S. Dunnett and M. Piacentini (eds) (2016), *Consumer Vulnerability: Conditions, Contexts and Characteristics*, London: Routledge.

Hamington, M. (2019), 'Integrating care ethics and design thinking', *Journal of Business Ethics*, **155** (1), 91–103.

Hanbury, M. (2018), 'Abercrombie came back from the dead by getting rid of its shirtless models and dark stores. Here's what else has changed for the retailer', accessed 7 December 2021 at www.businessinsider.com/abercrombie-makes -comeback-no-shirtless-models-dark-stores-2018-11?r=US&IR=T

Hanson, S. (2003), 'Geographical and feminist perspectives on entrepreneurship', *Geographische Zeitschrift*, **91** (1), 1–23.

Harju, A. A. and A. Huovinen (2015), 'Fashionably voluptuous: Normative femininity and resistant performative tactics in fatshion blogs', *Journal of Marketing Management*, **31** (15–16), 1602–1625.

Hasan, M. K., M. J. Hayek, W. A. Williams, S. Pane-Haden and M. P. M. Gelvez (2020), 'Activist identity construction of Madam C. J. Walker', *Journal of Management History*, **26** (3), 335–351.

Hawkins, R. (2011), 'One Pack = One Vaccine = one global motherhood? A feminist analysis of ethical consumption', *Gender, Place and Culture*, **18** (02), 235–253.

Hearn, J. and W. Hein (2015), 'Reframing gender and feminist knowledge construction in marketing and consumer research: Missing feminisms and the case of men and masculinities', *Journal of Marketing Management*, **31** (15–16), 1626–1651.

Heath, T., L. O'Malley, M. Heath and V. Story (2016), 'Caring and conflicted: Mothers' ethical judgments about consumption', *Journal of Business Ethics*, **136** (2), 237–250.

Hein, W., L. Steinfield, N. Ourahmoune, C. Coleman, L. T. Zayer and J. Littlefield (2016), 'Gender justice and the market: A transformative consumer research perspective', *Journal of Public Policy & Marketing*, **35** (2), 223–236.

Hern, A. (2020), 'Amazon closed French warehouses after court ruling on coronavirus', accessed 24 November 2021 at www.theguardian.com/technology/2020/apr/15/amazon-to-close-french-warehouses-over-coronavirus-concerns

Herring, S. (1993), 'Gender and democracy in computer mediated communication', *Electronic Journal of Communication*, **3** (2).

Hess, A. C. and V. Melnyk (2016), 'Pink or blue? The impact of gender cues on brand perceptions', *European Journal of Marketing*, **50** (9-10), 1550-1574.

Hetherington, K. (1997), *The Badlands of Modernity: Heterotopia and Social Ordering*, New York: Routledge.

Heyrick, E. (1828), *Appeal to the Hearts and Consciences of British Women*, Leicester: A. Cockshaw.

Hiken, A. (2021), 'Olay takes on computer algorithms to fight biased beauty standards', accessed 10 December 2021 at www.marketingdive.com/news/olay-takes-on-computer-algorithms-to-fight-biased-beauty-standards/606509/

Hilton, M. (2003), *Consumerism in Twentieth-century Britain: The Search for a Historical Movement*, Cambridge: Cambridge University Press.

Hirschman, E. C. (1993), 'Ideology in consumer research 1980 and 1990: A Marxist and feminist critique', *Journal of Consumer Research*, **19** (4), 537–555.

Hochschild, A. R. (1983), *The Managed Heart: Commercialization of Human Feeling*, Berkeley: University of California Press.

Hochschild, A. R. (2015), 'Global care chains and emotional surplus value', in D. Engster and T. Metz (eds), *Justice, Politics, and the Family*, New York: Routledge, pp. 249–261.

Hocks, M. E. (1999), 'Feminist interventions in electronic environments', *Computers and Composition*, **16** (1), 107–119.

Holt, D. B. and C. J. Thompson, (2004), 'Man-of-action heroes: The pursuit of heroic masculinity in everyday consumption', *Journal of Consumer Research*, **31** (2), 425–440.

hooks, b. (1981), *Ain't I a Woman: Black Women and Feminism*, Boston, MA: South End Press.

hooks, b. (1984), *Feminist Theory: From Margin to Center*, Boston, MA: South End Press.

hooks, b. (1992), *Black Looks: Race and Representation*, Boston, MA: South End Press.

Hopton, J. (1999), 'Militarism, masculinism and managerialism in the British Public Sector', *Journal of Gender Studies*, **8** (1), 71–82.

Horton, A. (2019), 'Financialization and non-disposable women: Real estate, debt and labour in UK care homes', *Environment and Planning A: Economy and Space*, DOI: 10.1177/0308518X19862580.

Hovorka, A. J. and D. Dietrich (2011), 'Entrepreneurship as a gendered process', *Entrepreneurship and Innovation*, **12** (1), 55–65.

Hoyt, E. E. (1926), *Primitive Trade: Its Psychology and Economics*, London: Kegan Paul.

Hoyt, E. E. (1928), *The Consumption of Wealth*, New York: Macmillan.

Hoyt, E. E. (1938), *Consumption in Our Society*, New York: McGraw Hill.

Hunt, K. (2010), 'The politics of food and women's neighborhood activism in first world war Britain', *International Labor and Working-Class History*, **77** (1), 8–26.

Hunt, S. D. and S. J. Vitell (1986), 'A general theory of marketing ethics', *Journal of Macromarketing*, **6** (1), 5–16.

Ibáñez, M. and E. García-Mingo (2021), 'Maping gendered social closure mechanisms through examination of seven male-dominated occupations', *Gender, Work and Organization*, forthcoming, DOI: 10.1111/gwao.12634.

Ignazio, C. D. and L. F. Klein (2020), *Data Feminism*, Cambridge, MA and London: The MIT Press.

Irigaray, L. (1985), *Speculum of the Other Woman*, trans. G. G. Gill, Ithaca, NY: Cornell University Press.

Jane, E. A. (2014), '"Your a ugly, whorish, slut": Understanding e-bile', *Feminist Media Studies*, **14** (4), 531–546.

Jauk, D. (2018), 'Of straddlers and rebels: Growing gender diversity among millennials is a fact', *Sex Roles*, **79** (11), 754–755.

Jeong, E. and J. Lee (2018), 'We take the red pill, we confront the DickTrix: Online feminist activism and the augmentation of gendered realities in South Korea', *Feminist Media Studies*, **18** (4), 705–717.

Jha, M. R. (2016), *The Global Beauty Industry: Colorism, Racism, and the National Body*, London: Routledge.

Jones, O. (2019), 'Woke-washing: How brands are cashing on the culture wars', accessed 18 November 2021 at www.theguardian.com/media/2019/may/23/woke-washing-brands-cashing-in-on-culture-wars-owen-jones

Jones, S. (2014), 'Gendered discourses of entrepreneurship in UK higher education: The fictive entrepreneur and the fictive student', *International Small Business Journal*, **32** (3), 237–258.

Joy, A. and A. Venkatesh (1994), 'Postmodernism, feminism, and the body: The visible and the invisible in consumer research', *International Journal of Research in Marketing*, **11** (4), 333–357.

Joy, A., R. W. Belk and R. Bhardwaj (2015), 'Judith Butler on performativity and precarity: Exploratory thoughts on gender and violence in India', *Journal of Marketing Management*, **31** (15–16), 1739–1745.

Juujärvia, S., L. Myyryb and K. Pessoa (2010), 'Does care reasoning make a difference? Relations between care, justice and dispositional empathy', *Journal of Moral Education*, **39** (4), 469–489.

Kao, F. H., B. S. Cheng, C. C. Kuo and M. P. Huang (2014), 'Stressors, withdrawal, and sabotage in frontline employees: The moderating effects of caring and service climates', *Journal of Occupational and Organizational Psychology*, **87** (4), 755–780.

Kates, S. M. (1999), 'Making the ad perfectly queer: Marketing "normality" to the gay men's community?', *Journal of Advertising*, **28** (1), 25–37.

Kates, S. M. (2000), 'Gay men on film: A typology of the scopophilic consumption pleasures of cultural text', *Consumption, Markets and Culture*, **4** (3), 281–313.

Kates, S. M. (2002), 'The protean quality of subcultural consumption: An ethnographic account of gay consumers', *Journal of Consumer Research*, **29** (3), 383–399.

Kates, S. M. (2003), 'Producing and consuming gendered representations: An interpretation of the Sydney Gay and Lesbian Mardi Gras', *Consumption, Markets and Culture*, **6** (1), 5–22.

Kendall, L. (1999), 'Recontextualizing "Cyberspace": Methodological considerations for on-line research', in S. Jones (ed.), *Doing Internet Research: Critical Issues and Methods for Examining the Net*, Thousand Oaks, CA: Sage, pp. 57–74.

Kilbourne, W. (2004), 'Sustainable communication and the dominant social paradigm: Can they be integrated?', *Marketing Theory*, **4** (3), 187–208.

Kilbourne, W. E., S. C. Beckmann and E. Thelen (2002), 'The role of the dominant social paradigm in environmental attitudes: A multinational examination', *Journal of Business Research*, **55** (3), 193–204.

Klein, M. (2014), *Helena Rubinstein: Beauty is Power*, Jewish Museum, New York: Yale University Press.

Knights, D. and T. Thanem (2005), 'Embodying emotional labour', in D. Morgan, B. Brandth and E. Kvande (eds), *Gender Bodies and Work*, London: Ashgate Publishing, pp. 31–43.

Knoll, S., M. Eisend and J. Steinhagen (2011), 'Gender roles in advertising: A comparison of gender stereotyping on public and private TV channels in Germany', *International Journal of Advertising*, **30** (5), 867–888.

Kohlberg, L. (1969), 'Stage and sequence: The cognitive development approach to socialization', in D. Goslin (ed.), *Handbook of Socialization Theory and Research*, Chicago, IL: Rand McNally, pp. 347–480.

Koman, R. G. (2006), 'Two American entrepreneurs: Madam C. J. Walker and J. C. Penney', *Organisation of American Historians Magazine of History*, **20** (1), 26–36.

Kotler, P. and G. Zaltman (1971), 'Social marketing: An approach to planned social change', *Journal of Marketing*, **35** (3), 3–12.

Kotz, E. (1992), 'The body you want: Liz Kotz interviews Judith Butler', *Artforum*, **31** (3), 82–89.

Kozinets, R. V. (2002), 'Can consumers escape the market? Emancipatory illuminations from Burning Man', *Journal of Consumer Research*, **29** (1), 20–38.

Kraemer, C. H. (2009), 'Gender essentialism in matriarchal Utopian fantasies: Are popular novels vehicles of sacred stories or purely propaganda?', *The Pomegranate*, **11** (2), 240–259.

Kravets, O., C. Preece and P. Maclaran (2020), 'The uniform entrepreneur: Making gender visible in social enterprise', *Journal of Macromarketing*, **40** (4), 445–458.

Krider, D. S. and P. G. Ross (1997), 'The experiences of women in a public relations firm: A phenomenological explication', *The Journal of Business Communication*, **34** (4), 437–454.

Kristeva, J. (1982), *Powers of Horror: An Essay on Abjection*, New York: Columbia University Press.

Krøtel, S. M. L., R. E. Ashworth and A. R. Villadsen (2019), 'Weakening the glass ceiling: Does organizational growth reduce gender segregation in the upper tiers of Danish local government?', *Public Management Review*, **21** (8), 1213–1235.

Kuruoğlu, A. P. (2022), 'Are all bodies knitworthy? Interrogating race and intersecting axes of marginalization in knitting space', in P. Maclaran, L. Stevens and O. Kravets (eds), *The Routledge Companion to Marketing and Feminism*, London: Routledge, pp. 241–256.

Kyrk, H. (1923), *A Theory of Consumption*, Boston, MA: Houghton Mifflin.

Lagesen, V. A. (2008), 'A cyberfeminist utopia? Perceptions of gender and computer science among Malaysian women computer science students and faculty', *Science, Technology, and Human Values*, **33** (1), 5–27.

Lareau, A. (2000), *Home Advantage: Social Class and Parental Intervention in Elementary Education*, New York: Rowman & Littlefield.

Legge, K. (1987), 'Women in personnel management: Uphill climb or downhill slide?', in A. Spencer and D. Podmore (eds), *In a Man's World: Essays on Women in Male-Dominated Professions*, London: Tavistock Publications, pp. 33–60.

Leneman, L. (1997), 'The awakened instinct: Vegetarianism and the women's suffrage movement in Britain', *Women's History Review*, **6** (2), 271–287.

Levitt, T. (1980), 'Marketing success through differentiation – of anything', *Harvard Business Review*, **58** (1), 83–91.

Levy, A (2005), *Female Chauvinist Pigs: Women and the Rise of Raunch Culture*, New York: Free Press.

Lewis, H. (2016), *The Politics of Everybody: Feminism, Queer Theory, and Marxism at the Intersection*, London: Zed Books.

Lewis, S. I. (2009), *Unexceptional Women: Female Proprietors in Mid-Nineteenth Century Albany, New York 1830–1885*, Columbus: The Ohio State University Press.

Liedermann, D. (2020), 'An investigation of the career progression experiences of women in mid and senior-level positions in Cape Town's public relations industry', Thesis (MTech (Public Relations Management)), Cape Peninsula University of Technology.

Littler, J. (2009), *Radical Consumption: Shopping for Change in Contemporary Culture*, Maidenhead: Open University Press.

Littler, J. (2017), *Against Meritocracy: Culture, Power and Myths of Mobility*, London and New York: Routledge.

Littler, J. and C. Rottenberg (2021), 'Feminist solidarities: Theoretical and practical complexitie's, *Gender, Work & Organization*, **28** (3), 864–877.

Lovelock, C. H., J. Wirtz and P. Chew (2009), *Essentials of Services Marketing*, London: Prentice Hall.

Lubar, S. (1998), 'Men/women/production/consumption', in R. Horowitz and A. Mohun (eds), *His and Hers: Gender Consumption and Technology*, Charlottesville: University of Virginia Press, pp. 7–37.

Lupton, B. (2000), 'Maintaining masculinity: Men who do "women's work"', *British Journal of Management*, **11** (s1), 33–48.

Lutkins, N. (2017), 'Time to give peace a chance in marketing language?', *Sales and Marketing Solutions* EMEA blog, 24 April, accessed 1 December 2021 at www.business.linkedin.com/en-uk/marketing-solutions/blog/posts/Marketing -Trends/2017/time-to-give-peace-a-chance-in-marketing-language

MacKinnon, C. (1987), *Feminism Unmodified: Discourses on Life and Law*, Cambridge, MA: Harvard University Press.

Maclaran, P. and M. Catterall (2000), 'Bridging the knowledge divide: Issues on the feminisation of marketing practice', *Journal of Marketing Management*, **16** (6), 635–646.

Maclaran, P. and O. Kravets (2018), 'Feminist perspectives in marketing: Past, present and future', in M. Tadajewski, J. Dengri-Knott and N. Dholakia (eds), *The Routledge Companion to Critical Marketing*, London: Routledge, pp. 64–82.

Maclaran, P. and C. Otnes (2017), 'Reinvigorating the Sherlock myth: Elementary gender-bending', in J. Sherry and E. Fischer (eds), *Contemporary Consumer Culture Theory*, London: Routledge, pp. 152–172.

Maclaran, P. and L. Stevens (2019), 'Thinking through feminist theorising: Poststructuralist feminism, ecofeminism and intersectionality', in S. Dobscha (ed.), *Handbook of Research on Gender and Marketing*', Cheltenham, UK and Northampton, MA, USA: Edward Elgar Publishing, pp. 229–251.

Maclaran, P., M. Catterall and L. Stevens (1997), 'The "glasshouse effect": Women in marketing management', *Marketing Intelligence and Planning*, **15** (7), 309–317.

Maclaran, P., M. Hogg, M. Catterall and R. Kozinets (2004), 'Gender, technology and computer-mediated communications in consumption-related online communities', in K. M. Ekström and H. Brembeck (eds), *Elusive Consumption*, Oxford: Berg, pp. 145–171.

Mahdawi, A. (2020), 'After the sleep economy, what's next to be monetised? Breathing?', accessed 24 November 2021 at www.theguardian.com/ commentisfree/2020/jan/15/after-the-sleep-economy-whats-next-to-be -monetised-breathing

Mann, N. R. (2012), *Glastonbury Tor: A Guide to the History and Legends*, Gardena, CA: SCB Distributors.

Marshall, D., T. Davis, M. K. Hogg, T. Schneider and A. Petersen (2014), 'From overt provider to invisible presence: Discursive shifts in advertising portrayals of the father in Good Housekeeping, 1950–2010', *Journal of Marketing Management*, **30** (15–16), 1654–1679.

Martin, D. M., J. W. Schouten and J. H. McAlexander (2006), 'Claiming the throttle: Multiple femininities in a hyper-masculine subculture', *Consumption, Markets and Culture*, **9** (3), 171–205.

Massey, D. (2013), 'Vocabularies of the economy', *Soundings*, **54** (54), 9–22.

McCracken, G. (1986), 'Culture and consumption: A theoretical account of the structure and movement of the cultural meaning of consumer goods', *Journal of Consumer Research*, **13** (1), 71–84.

McDonagh, P. and A. Prothero (1997), 'Leap-frog marketing: The contribution of ecofeminist thought to the world of patriarchal marketing', *Marketing Intelligence and Planning*, **15** (7), 361–368.

McDonald, M. G. (2000), 'The marketing of the Women's National Basketball Association and the making of postfeminism', *International Review for the Sociology of Sport*, **35** (1), 35–47.

McDowell, L. (2003), *Redundant Masculinities*, Oxford: Blackwell.

McIlwee, J. S. and G. J. Robinson (1992), *Women in Engineering: Gender, Power and Workplace Culture*, Albany, NY: SUNY Press.

McRobbie, A. (1997), 'Bridging the gap: Feminism, fashion and consumption', *Feminist Review*, **55**, 73–89.

McRobbie, A. (2015), 'Notes on the perfect: Competitive femininity in neoliberal times', *Australian Feminist Studies*, **30** (83), 3–20.

McVey, L., L. Gurrieri and M. Tyler (2018), 'The structural oppression of women by markets: The continuum of sexual violence and the online pornography market', *Journal of Marketing Management*, **37** (1–2), 40–67.

Midgley, C. (1996), *Women Against Slavery: The British Campaigns, 1780–1870*, New York: Routledge.

Midgley, C. (2007), *Feminism and Empire: Women Activists in Imperial Britain, 1790–1865*, London: Routledge.

Miles, S. (2010), *Spaces for Consumption*, Los Angeles: Sage.

Miller, D. (ed.) (1998), *Material Cultures: Why Some Things Matter*, Chicago: University of Chicago Press.

Miller, D. (2012), *Consumption and Its Consequences*, Cambridge: Polity.

Moisio, R., E. J. Arnould and J. W. Gentry (2013), 'Productive consumption in the class-mediated construction of domestic masculinity: Do-it-yourself (DIY) home improvement in men's identity work', *Journal of Consumer Research*, **40** (2), 298–316.

Moisio, R., E. J. Arnould and L. L. Price (2004), 'Between mothers and markets: Constructing family identity through homemade food', *Journal of Consumer Culture*, **4** (3), 361–384.

Mol, A. (2008), *The Logic of Care: Health and the Problem of Patient Choice*, London and New York: Routledge.

Moore, N. (2015), 'Eco/feminist genealogies: Renewing promises and new possibilities', in M. Phillips and N. Rumens (eds), *Contemporary Perspectives on Ecofeminism*, London: Routledge, pp. 19–37.

Mort, F. (2013), *Cultures of Consumption*, London: Routledge.

Mulvey, L. (1975), 'Visual pleasure and narrative cinema', *Screen*, **16** (3), 6–18.

Muniz, A. M. and T. C. O'Guinn (2001), 'Brand community', *Journal of Consumer Research*, **27** (4), 412–432.

Nelson, J. A. (1999), 'Of markets and martyrs: Is It OK to pay well for care?', *Feminist Economics*, **5** (3), 43–59.

Newholm, T. and S. Newholm (2016), 'Consumption ethics in history', in D. Shaw, M. Carrington and A. Chatzidakis (eds), *Ethics and Morality in Consumption: Interdisciplinary Perspectives*, London: Routledge, pp. 97–115.

Newton, M., M. Fry, D. Watson, L. Gano-Overway, M. S. Kim, M. Magyar and M. Guivernau (2007), 'Psychometric properties of the caring climate scale in a physical activity setting', *Revista de Psicología del Deporte*, **16** (1), 67–84.

Nicholson, J. and E. Kurucz (2019), 'Relational leadership for sustainability: Building an ethical framework from the moral theory of "ethics of care"', *Journal of Business Ethics*, **156** (1), 25–43.

Nixon, D. (2009), '"I can't put a smiley face on": Working-class masculinity, emotional labour and service work in the new economy', *Gender, Work and Organisation*, **16** (3), 300–322.

Noddings, N. (2003), *Caring: A Feminine Approach to Ethics and Moral Education, Second Edition*, Berkeley: University of California.

Noddings, N. (2015), 'Care ethics and "caring" organizations', in D. Engster and M. Hamington (eds), *Care Ethics and Political Theory*, Oxford: Oxford University Press, pp. 72–84.

Nolke, A. (2018), 'Making diversity conform? An intersectional, longitudinal analysis of LGBT-specific mainstream media advertisements', *Journal of Homosexuality*, **65** (2), 224–255.

Norgaard, K.M., 1998. The essentialism of ecofeminism and the real. *Organization & Environment*, *11*(4), pp.492-497.

Oakenfull, G. K. (2012), 'Gay consumers and brand usage: The gender-flexing role of gay identity', *Psychology and Marketing*, **29** (12), 968–979.

Oakenfull, G. K. and T. B. Greenlee (2005), 'Queer eye for a gay guy: Using market-specific symbols in advertising to attract gay consumers without alienating the mainstream', *Psychology and Marketing*, **22** (5), 421–439.

Oakley, A. (1972), *Sex, Gender, and Society*, New York: Harper Colophon.

O'Malley, L. and C. Tynan (1999), 'The utility of the relationship metaphor in consumer markets: A critical evaluation', *Journal of Marketing Management*, **15** (7), 587–602.

Otnes, C. and E. Fischer (2022), 'Feminist brands: What are they and what's the matter with them?', in P. Maclaran, L. Stevens and O. Kravets (eds), *The Routledge Companion to Marketing and Feminism*, London: Routledge, pp. 75–89.

Oudshoorn, N., R. Saetnan and M. Lie (2002), 'On gender and things: Reflections on an exhibition on gendered artefacts', *Women's Studies International Forum*, **25** (4), 471–483.

Ourahmoune, N. and H. El Jurdi (2022), 'Marketing and the missing feminisms: Decolonial feminism and the Arab Spring', in P. Maclaran, L. Stevens and O. Kravets (eds), *The Routledge Companion to Marketing and Feminism*, London: Routledge, pp. 257–267.

Paaßen, B., T. Morgenroth and M. Stratemeyer (2017), 'What is a true gamer? The male gamer stereotype and the marginalisation of women in video game culture', *Sex Roles*, **76** (7–8), 421–435.

Pacey, A. (1983), *The Culture of Technology*, Cambridge, MA: The MIT Press.

Paoletti, J. B. (2012), *Pink and Blue: Telling the Boys From the Girls in America*, Bloomington: Indiana University Press.

Paranque, B. and H. Willmott (2014), 'Cooperatives – Saviours or gravediggers of capitalism? Critical performativity and the John Lewis Partnership', *Organization*, **21** (5), 604–625.

Parkinson, H. J. (2014), 'PornHub can't keep it up: Huge New York billboard ad taken down', accessed 18 November 2021 at www.theguardian.com/ technology/2014/oct/09/pornhub-times-square-new-york-billboard

Parsons, E. (2013), 'Pioneering consumer economist: Elizabeth Ellis Hoyt (1893–1980)', *Journal of Historical Research in Marketing*, **5** (3), 334–350.

Parsons, E., T. Kearney, E. Surman, B. Cappellini, S. Moffat, V. Harman and K. Scheurenbrand (2021), 'Who really cares? Introducing an "Ethics of Care" to debates on transformative value co-creation', *Journal of Business Research*, **122**, 794–804.

Patterson, M. and R. Elliott (2002), 'Negotiating masculinities: Advertising and the inversion of the male gaze', *Consumption, Markets & Culture*, **5** (3), 231–249.

Paxton, D. L. (1999), 'Marion Zimmer Bradley and *The Mists of Avalon*', *Arthuriana*, **9** (1), 110–126.

Penny, L. (2010), *Meat Market: Female Flesh under Capitalism*, Winchester: Zero Books.

Pepper, J. (2018), 'Glastonbury, the hippie's Vale of Avalon – Archive, 1969', accessed 24 November at www.theguardian.com/music/2018/dec/20/ glastonbury-the-hippies-vale-of-avalon-archive-1969

Pezzutto, S. (2019), 'From porn performer to porntropreneur: Online entrepreneurship, social media branding, and selfhood in contemporary trans pornography', *International Journal of Gender Studies*, **8** (16), 30–60.

Plant, S. (1995), 'The future looms: Weaving women and cybernetics', *Body and Society*, **1** (3–4), 45–64.

Plumwood, V. (1993), *Feminism and the Mastery of Nature*, London: Routledge.

Possamai, A. (1999), 'Diversity in alternative spiritualities: Keeping New Age at bay', *Australian Religion Studies Review*, **12** (2), 111–124.

Povich, L. (2015), 'Lilian Vernon, creator of a bustling catalog business, dies at 88', *The New York Times*, 14 December.

Powers, K. (2019), 'Shattering gendered marketing', accessed 18 November 2021 at www.ama.org/marketing-news/shattering-gendered-marketing

Puntoni, S., S. Sweldens and N. T. Tavassoli (2011), 'Gender identity salience and perceived vulnerability to breast cancer', *Journal of Marketing Research*, **48** (3), 413–424.

Rakow, L. F. (1992), *Gender on the Line: Women, the Telephone and Community Life*, Urbana and Chicago: University of Illinois Press.

Rawlinson, K. (2018), 'British people do more than £1tn of housework each year – unpaid', accessed 24 November 2021 at www.theguardian.com/society/ 2018/oct/03/british-people-do-more-than-1-trillion-of-housework-each-year -unpaid

Razavi, S. (2007), 'The political and social economy of care in a development context: Conceptual issues, research questions and policy options', *Gender and*

Development Programme Paper Number 3, Geneva: United Nations Research Institute for Social Development.

Rinallo, D. (2007), 'Metro/fashion/tribes of men: Negotiating the boundaries of men's legitimate consumption', in R. V. Kozinets, B. Cova and A. Shankar (eds), *Consumer Tribes*, Oxford: Butterworth-Heinemann, pp. 76–92.

Roberts, L. D. and M. R. Parks (2001), 'The social geography of genderswitching in virtual environments on the internet', in E. Green and A. Adam (eds), *Virtual Gender: Technologies, Consumption and Gender*, London: Routledge, pp. 265–285.

Robinson, H. (2020), 'The Playboy logo: Can we separate the brand from its baggage', accessed 18 November 2021 at www.redbrick.me/the-playboy-logo -can-we-separate-the-brand-from-its-baggage

Rome, A. (2022), 'Taking off the blindfold: The perils of pornification and sexual abjectification', in P. Maclaran, L. Stevens and O. Kravets (eds), *The Routledge Companion to Marketing and Feminism*, London: Routledge, pp. 206–221.

Rommes, E., E. Van Osst and N. Oudshoorn (2001), 'Gender in the design of the digital city of Amsterdam', in E. Green and A. Adam (eds), *Virtual Gender: Technologies, Consumption and Gender*, London: Routledge, pp. 241–262.

Roos, P. A. and J. E. Manley (1996), 'Staffing personnel: Feminization and change in human resource management', *Sociological Focus*, **29** (3), 245–261.

Ross, P. (2018), 'Pagan paradise: Glastonbury without the festival', accessed 24 November 2021 at www.theguardian.com/travel/2018/jun/22/glastonbury -town-festival-druids-pagans-travel-holidays

Rottenberg, C. (2014), 'The rise of neoliberal feminism', *Cultural Studies*, **28** (3), 418–437.

Rottenberg, C. (2018), *The Rise of Neoliberal Feminism*, Oxford: Oxford University Press.

Rowe, S. and D. Rowe (2015), 'The politics of in/appropriate/d others: Moving beyond the vulnerable consumer in the LBGT market/movement', in C. Schultz, R. Benton and O. Kravets (eds), *Proceedings of the 40th Macromarketing Conference*, Chicago: Quinlan School of Business, pp. 736–739.

Ruether, R. R. (1975), 'Home and work: Women's roles and the transformation of values', *Theological Studies*, **36** (4), 647–659.

Rumens, N. (2017), *Queer Business: Queering Organization Sexualities*, London and New York: Routledge.

Russell, H. (2021), 'Everyone is awesome: Lego to launch first LGBTQ+ set', accessed 18 November 2021 at www.theguardian.com/world/2021/may/20/ everyone-is-awesome-lego-launch-first-lgbtq-set

Sandberg, S. (2013), *Lean in: Women, Work, and the Will to Lead*, New York: Alfred A. Knopf.

Sandel, M. J. (2012), *What Money Can't Buy: The Moral Limits of Markets*, London: Macmillan.

Sargisson, L. (1996), *Contemporary Feminist Utopianism*, London: Routledge.

Sargisson, L. (2001), 'What's wrong with ecofeminism?', *Environmental Politics*, **10** (1), 52–64.

Scanlon, J. (2013), '"A dozen ideas to the minute": Advertising women, advertising to women', *Journal of Historical Research in Marketing*, **5** (3), 273–290.

Schouten, J. W. and J. H. McAlexander (1995), 'Subcultures of consumption: An ethnography of the new bikers', *Journal of Consumer Research*, **22** (1), 43–61.

Schroeder, J. E. and D. Zwick (2004), 'Mirrors of masculinity: Representation and identity in advertising images', *Consumption, Markets and Culture*, **7** (1), 21–52.

Schumpeter, J. A. (1934), *The Theory of Economic Development: An Inquiry into Profits, Capital, Credit, Interest, and the Business Cycle*, New Brunswick, NJ: Transaction Publishers.

Scott, L. M. (1992), 'Playing with pictures: Postmodernism, poststructuralism and advertising visuals', in J. Sherry and B. Sternthal (eds), *Advances in Consumer Research Volume 19*, Provo, UT: Association for Consumer Research, pp. 843–849.

Scott, L. M. (2005), *Fresh Lipstick: Redressing Fashion and Feminism*, New York: Palgrave.

Scott, L. M. (2006), 'Market feminism: The case for a paradigm shift', *Advertising & Society Review*, **7** (2).

Scott, L. (2020), *The Double X Economy: The Epic Potential of Empowering Women*, New York: Farrar, Straus and Giroux.

Scott, L. and P. Maclaran (2012), 'Consuming the mists and myths of Avalon: A case study of pilgrimage in Glastonbury', in D. Rinallo, L. Scott and P. Maclaran (eds), *Consumption and Spirituality*, London: Routledge, pp. 211–224.

Scott, L., C. Dolan, M. Johnstone-Louis, K. Sugden and M. Wu (2012), 'Enterprise and inequality: The case of Avon in South Africa', *Journal of Entrepreneurship Theory and Practice*, **36** (3), 543–568.

Segal, L. (1993), 'False promises: Anti-pornography feminism', in R. Milliband and L. Panitch (eds), *Real Problems, False Solutions: Socialist Register 1993*, London: Merlin Press.

Segal, L. (2017), *Making Trouble: Life and Politics*, London: Verso Books.

Segran, E. (2019), 'Coca-Cola, Nestle and PespsiCo are the world's biggest plastic polluters – again', accessed 28 November 2021 at www.fastcompany.com/90425011/coca-cola-nestle-and-pepsico-are-the-worlds-biggest-plastic-polluters-again

Sexton, D. and P. Haberman (1974), 'Women in magazine advertisements', *Journal of Advertising Research*, **14** (4), 41–46.

Shaw, D. and T. Newholm (2002), 'Voluntary simplicity and the ethics of consumption', *Psychology and Marketing*, **19** (2), 167–185.

Shaw, D., M. Carrington and A. Chatzidakis (eds) (2016), *Ethics and Morality in Consumption: Interdisciplinary Perspectives*, London: Routledge.

Shields, S. A. (2008), 'Gender: An intersectionality perspective', *Sex Roles*, **59** (5), 301–311.

Skeggs, B. (1997), *Formations of Class and Gender: Becoming Respectable*, London: Sage.

Skeggs, B. (2014), 'Values beyond value? Is anything beyond the logic of capital?', *The British Journal of Sociology*, **65** (1), 1–20.

Slaughter, A. (2012), 'Why women still can't have it all', *The Atlantic*, July/August.

Sobande, F. (2019), 'Woke-washing: "Intersectional" femvertising and branding "woke" bravery, *European Journal of Marketing*, **54** (11), 2723–2745.

Sobande, F. (2022), 'Black women's digital media and marketplace experiences: Between buying, branding, and Black Lives Matter', in P. Maclaran, L. Stevens and O. Kravets (eds), *The Routledge Companion to Marketing and Feminism*, London: Routledge, pp. 339–348.

Soja, E. W. (1996), *Thirdspace: Journeys to Los Angeles and Other Real – and – Imagined Places*, Cambridge, MA: Blackwell.

Southern, R. and E. Harmer (2021), 'Twitter, incivility and "everyday" gendered othering: An analysis of tweets sent to UK Members of Parliament', *Social Science Computer Review*, 39 (2), 259–275.

Spender, D. (1995), *Nattering on the Net: Women, Power and Cyberspace*, North Melbourne: Spinifex.

Spiess, L. and P. Waring (2005), 'Aesthetic labour, cost minimisation and the labour process in the Asia Pacific airline industry', *Employee Relations*, **27** (2), 193–207.

Spruill, W. G. and C. W. Wootton (1995), 'The struggle of women in accounting: The Case of Jennie Palen, pioneer accountant, historian and poet', *Critical Perspectives on Accounting*, **6** (4), 371–389.

Starhawk (1979), *The Spiral Dance: A Rebirth of the Ancient Religion of the Great Goddess*, San Francisco, CA: Harper and Row.

Steinfield, L. (2021), '1,2,3,4, I declare … empowerment? A material-discursive analysis of the marketisation, measurement and marketing of women's economic empowerment', *Journal of Marketing Management*, **37** (3–4), 320–356.

Steinfield, L., C. Coleman, L. Tuncay Zayer, N. Ourahmoune and W. Hein (2019), '"Power logics of consumers" gendered (in)justices: Reading reproductive health interventions through the transformative gender justice framework', *Consumption Markets and Culture*, **22** (4), 406–429.

Stern, B. B. (1993), 'Feminist literary criticism and the deconstruction of ads: A postmodern view of advertising and consumer responses', *Journal of Consumer Research*, **19** (4), 556–566.

Stern, B. B. and M. B. Holbrook (1994), 'Gender and genre in the interpretation of advertising text', in J. A. Costa (ed.), *Gender Issues and Consumer Behavior*, Thousand Oaks, CA: Sage, pp. 11–47.

Stevens, L. (2018), 'Gender, marketing, and emotions: A critical, feminist exploration of the ideological helix that defines our working worlds', in M. Tadajewski, M. Higgins, J. Denegri-Knott and R. Varman (eds), *Routledge Companion to Critical Marketing*, London: Routledge, pp. 415–429.

Stevens, L. and P. Maclaran (2000), 'The spectacle and the speculum: Voyeurism and women's consumption of magazines', in C. Otnes (ed.), *GCB – Gender and Consumer Behavior Volume 5*, Urbana, IL: Association for Consumer Research, pp. 19–32.

Stevens, L. and P. Maclaran (2008), 'The carnal feminine: Women, advertising and consumption', in S. Borghini, M. A. McGrath and C. Otnes (eds), *European Advances in Consumer Research Volume 8*, Duluth, MN: Association for Consumer Research, pp. 169–174.

Stevens, L., B. Cappellini and G. Smith (2015), 'Nigellissima: A study of glamour, performativity, and embodiment', *Journal of Marketing Management*, **31** (5–6), 1–22.

Stevens, L., M. Kearney and P. Maclaran (2013), 'Uddering the other: Androcentrism, ecofeminism, and the dark side of anthropomorphic marketing', *Journal of Marketing Management*, **29** (1–2), 158–174.

Stevens, L., P. Maclaran and M. Kearney (2014), 'Boudoirs, cowdillacs and rotolactors: A salutary tale of Elsie the brand mascot', in S. Brown and S. Ponsonby-McCabe (eds), *Brand Mascots: And Other Marketing Animals*, London: Routledge, pp. 110–122.

Streeck, W. (2012), 'Citizens as customers: Considerations on the new politics of consumption', *New Left Review*, **76**, 27–47.

Tadajewski, M. (2013), 'Helen Woodward and Hazel Kyrk: Economic radicalism, consumption symbolism and female contributions to marketing theory and advertising practice', *Journal of Historical Research in Marketing*, **5** (3), 385–412.

Tadajewski, M. and P. Maclaran (2013), 'Editorial: Remembering female contributors to marketing theory, thought and practice', *Journal of Historical Research in Marketing*, **5** (3), 260–272.

Taylor, L. (1996), 'Food riots revisited', *Journal of Social History*, **30** (2), 483–496.

The Care Collective (2020), *The Care Manifesto*, London: Verso Books.

Thompson, C. J. and T. Üstüner (2015), 'Women skating on the edge: Marketplace performances as ideological edgework', *Journal of Consumer Research*, **42** (2), 235–265.

Thompson-Whiteside, H. (2020), 'Something in Adland doesn't add up: It's time to make female creatives count', *Business Horizons*, **63** (5), 597–606.

Tienari, J., S. Quack and H. Theobald (1999), 'Managerial "mommy tracks": Feminisation of middle management in German and Finnish banking', paper presented to the Gender, Management and Organisation Stream, Critical Management Studies Conference, University of Manchester, UK, 14–16 July.

Toupin, S. (2014), 'Feminist hackerspaces: The synthesis of feminist and hacker cultures', *Journal of Peer Production*, **5** (2014), 1–11.

Tronto, J. C. (1993), *Moral Boundaries: A Political Argument For an Ethic of Care*, New York: Routledge.

Tronto, J. C. (2013), *Caring Democracy: Markets, Equality, and Justice*, New York: New York University Press.

Trump, I. (2017), *Women Who Work: Rewriting the Rules for Success*, New York: Penguin.

Tsai, W.-H. S. (2010), 'Assimilating the queers: Representations of gay men, bisexual and transgender people in mainstream advertising', *Advertising & Society Review*, 11 (1).

Turkle, S. (1986), 'Computational reticence: Why women fear the intimate machine', in C. Kramarae (ed.), *Technology and Women's Voice: Keeping in Touch*, New York: Routledge, pp. 41–61.

Tynan, C. (1997), 'A review of the marriage analogy in relationship marketing', *Journal of Marketing Management*, **13** (7), 695–704.

Valtonen, A. and E. Närvänen (2015), 'Gendered reading of the body in the bed', *Journal of Marketing Management*, **31** (15–16), 1583–1601.

Varman, R., P. Goswami and D. Vijay (2018), 'The precarity of respectable consumption: Normalising sexual violence against women', *Journal of Marketing Management*, **34** (11–12), 932–964.

Victor, B. and J. B. Cullen (1988), 'The organizational bases of ethical work climates', *Administrative Science Quarterly*, **33** (1), 101–125.

Vredenburg, J., S. Kapitan, A. Spry and J. A. Kemper (2020), 'Brands taking a stand: Authentic brand activism or woke washing?', *Journal of Public Policy and Marketing*, **39** (4), 444–460.

Wagner, L. and J. Banos (1973), 'A woman's place: A follow-up analysis of the roles portrayed by women in magazine advertisements', *Journal of Marketing Research*, **10** (5), 213–214.

Wajcman, J. (2000), 'Reflections on gender and technology studies: In what state is the art?', *Social Studies of Sciences*, **30** (3), 447–464.

Wajcman, J. (2010), 'Feminist theories of technology', *Cambridge Journal of Economics*, **34** (1), 143–152.

Wallowitz, L. (2008), 'Resisting the white gaze: Critical literacy and Toni Morrison's "The Bluest Eye"', in L. Wallowitz (ed.), *Counterpoints Volume 326: Critical Literacy as Resistance: Teaching for Social Justice Across the Secondary Curriculum*, Peter Lang AG, pp. 151–164.

Walters, K. (2016), 'Mall models: How Abercrombie & Fitch sexualizes its retail workers', *Sexualisation, Media and Society*, **2** (2), 1–5.

Warren, K. (2000), *Ecofeminist Philosophy: A Western Perspective on What It Is and Why It Matters*, Lanham, MD: Rowman & Littlefield.

Weedon, C. (1987). *Feminist Practice and Post-structuralist Theory*, London: Basil Blackwell.

West, C. (1996), 'Goffman in feminist perspective', *Sociological Perspectives*, **39** (3), 353–369.

White, M. (2001), 'Visual pleasure in textual places: Gazing in multi-user object-oriented worlds', in E. Green and A. Adam (eds), *Virtual Gender: Technologies, Consumption and Gender*, London: Routledge, pp. 124–149.

Williams, F. (2001), 'In and beyond New Labour: Towards a new political ethic of care', *Critical Social Policy*, **21** (4), 467–493.

Winch, A. (2015), 'Brand intimacy, female friendship and digital surveillance networks', *New Formations*, **84–85**, 228–245.

Windels, K., S. Champlin, S. Shelton, Y. Sterbenk and M. Poteet (2020), 'Selling feminism: How female empowerment campaigns employ postfeminist discourses', *Journal of Advertising*, **49** (1), 18–33.

Witkowski, T. H. (2017), *A History of American Consumption: Threads of Meaning, Gender, and Resistance*, London and New York: Routledge.

Wittig, M. (1980), *The Straight Mind and Other Essays*, New York: Harvester Wheatsheaf.

Witz, A., C. Warhurst and D. Nickson (2003), 'The labour of aesthetics and the aesthetics of organization', *Organization*, **10** (1), 33–54.

Yates, S. J. and K. Littleton (2001), 'Understanding computer game cultures: A situated approach', in E. Green and A. Adam (eds), *Virtual Gender: Technologies, Consumption and Gender*, London: Routledge, pp. 103–123.

Zayer, L. T. and C. Coleman, (2015), 'Advertising professionals' perceptions of the impact of gender portrayals on men and women: A question of ethics?', *Journal of Advertising*, **44** (3), 1–12.

Zayer, L. T. and C. Otnes (2012), 'Climbing the ladder or chasing a dream? Men's responses to idealized portrayals of masculinity in advertising', in C. Otnes and L. T. Zayer (eds), *Gender, Culture, and Consumer Behavior*, New York: Routledge, pp. 87–110.

Zayer, L. T., K. Sredl, M. Parmentier and C. Coleman (2012), 'Consumption and gender identity in popular media: Discourses of domesticity, authenticity, and sexuality', *Consumption Markets and Culture*, **15** (4), 333–357.

Ziv, A. (2015), *Explicit Utopias: Rewriting the Sexual in Women's Pornography*, Albany, NY: SUNY Press.

Zuckerman, M. E. and M. L. Carsky (1990), 'Contribution of women to U.S. marketing thought: The consumers' perspective, 1900–1940', *Journal of the Academy of Marketing Science*, **18** (4), 313–317.

Zuckerman, M. E. and M. L. Carsky (1992), 'Feminist theory and marketing thought: Toward a new approach for consumer research', in J. F. Sherry Jr. and B. Sternthal (eds), *NA – Advances in Consumer Research Volume 19*, Provo, UT: Association for Consumer Research, pp. 464–471.

Index

Printed and bound by CPI Group (UK) Ltd, Croydon, CR0 4YY

16/04/2025

14658492-0001